Archival futures

Edited by
Caroline Brown

facet
publishing

Published by Facet Publishing,
7 Ridgmount Street, London WC1E 7AE
www.facetpublishing.co.uk

Facet Publishing is wholly owned by CILIP: the Library and
Information Association.

British Library Cataloguing in Publication Data
A catalogue record for this book is available from the British Library.

ISBN 978-1-78330-182-9 (paperback)
ISBN 978-1-78330-218-5 (hardback)
ISBN 978-1-78330-219-2 (e-book)

First published 2018

Text printed on FSC accredited material.

Typeset from editors' files by Flagholme Publishing Services in 10/13pt
Palatino and OpenSans
Printed and made in Great Britain by CPI Group (UK) Ltd, Croydon,
CR0 4YY.

Archival futures

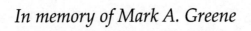
In memory of Mark A. Greene

Contents

Notes on contributors

Caroline Brown is Programme Leader for the distance learning archives and family history programmes at the University of Dundee, Scotland. She is also University Archivist and an assistant director in the Library & Learning Centre and Culture & Information at the University. She has authored articles and chapters on archival themes as well as edited a book for Facet Publishing, *Archives and Recordkeeping: theory into practice* (2014). She has served on several professional and academic bodies and is currently a Trustee of the Scottish Council on Archives and a Director of the Scottish Archive Network.

Jenny Bunn is a Lecturer and Programme Director for the MA in Archives and Records Management at University College London (UCL). She has previously worked for the V&A Museum, The Royal Bank of Scotland and The National Archives. She is actively involved with the work of the Archives and Records Association as part of the editorial team for *Archives and Records* and as a member of the Committee of the Section for Archives and Technology. Her research and teaching interests focus on the evolution of the archival profession in its ongoing interaction with all forms of technology.

Luciana Duranti is Professor of Archival Science and Diplomatics in the masters and doctoral archival degree programmes at the University of British Columbia, Canada. She is Director of the Centre for the International Study of Contemporary Records and Archives and InterPARES, the largest and longest living publicly funded research project on the preservation of authentic electronic records (1998–2019). She is the President of the Association of Canadian Archivists (2016–2018).

Joanne Evans, Associate Professor, is an ARC Future Fellow in the Faculty of IT at Monash University, Australia. She is co-ordinator of the Records Continuum Research Group and her research relates to the design and development of recordkeeping and archiving systems, with particular emphasis on participatory recordkeeping models, interoperability and sustainability.

Dr Craig Gauld is a Lecturer in Archive and Information Studies, Centre for Archive and Information Studies (CAIS), at the University of Dundee in Scotland. He is a qualified archivist and has worked at the University of Strathclyde Archives, Ayrshire Archives and Shetland Archives. He has a PhD from the University of Glasgow on archival theory and is Distance Learning Officer for the School of Humanities. He carries out research into recordkeeping theory, the role of the archivist in the 21st century and how the changing nature of information threatens the archival profession as it has been traditionally understood. Publications include Democratising or Privileging: the democratisation of knowledge and the role of the archivist, *Archival Science* (2017).

Victoria Lemieux is Associate Professor of Archival Science at the University of British Columbia, Canada, and founder of the Blockchain@UBC research and education cluster. Her research focuses on risk to the availability of trustworthy records and how these risks impact. She holds a doctorate from University College London (Archival Studies, 2002) and since 2005 has been a Certified Information Systems Security Professional (CISSP). She is also winner of the 2015 Emmett Leahy Award for outstanding contributions to the field of records management, a 2015 World Bank Big Data Innovation Award and a 2016 Emerald Literati Award for her research on blockchain technology.

Michael Moss is an Emeritus Professor in the iSchool at Northumbria University, UK. He is recognised as an authority on the transition from the analogue to the digital environment in archival sciences. He was a member of the Lord Chancellor's Advisory Council on Records and Archives and was awarded a lifetime achievement award by the All Party Parliamentary Committee on History and Records in 2017. He is a member of Columbia University's History Lab's global challenge project which is exploring the ingest and use of born-digital records. His recent publications include with Tim Gollins, Our Digital Legacy: an archival perspective, *Journal of Contemporary Archival Studies* (2017); with David Thomas, Overlapping Temporalities – the judge, the historian and the citizen, *Archives* (2017); Understanding Core Business Records in Alison Turton (ed.), *International Business Records* (2017); and Memory Institutions, the Archive and Digital Disruption? in Andrew Hoskins (ed.), *Digital Memory Studies* (2017).

Gillian Oliver is Associate Professor of Information Management and Director of the Centre for Organisational and Social Informatics at Monash University, Australia. Previous academic and practice roles were in information management in the UK, Germany and New Zealand.

Sonia Ranade is Head of Digital Archiving at The National Archives. Her research interests include probabilistic approaches to archival description, new models for access to digital archives, and computational techniques for records linking and contextualisation. She holds a PhD in Information Science from the University of Sheffield in the UK.

Barbara Reed has been a consultant in the fields of records, archives and information management since 1985. She is active in professional arenas, including teaching and training. She has played a major role in the development of Australian and International standards for records management, digitisation and recordkeeping metadata.

Kate Theimer is the author of the popular blog *ArchivesNext* and a frequent writer, speaker and commentator on issues related to the future of archives. She is the editor of the series *Innovative Practices for Archives & Special Collections*. She edited *A Different Kind of Web: new connections between archives and our users* (2011), and contributed chapters to *Many Happy Returns: advocacy for archives and archivists* (2011), *The Future of Archives and Recordkeeping* (2010) and the *Encyclopedia of Archival Science* (2015). Kate served on the Council of the Society of American Archivists from 2010 to 2013. Before starting her career as an independent writer and editor, she worked in the policy division of the National Archives and Records Administration.

David Thomas joined Northumbria University in the UK in 2014 as a Visiting Professor, having spent most of his career at the UK National Archives where he was Head of IT and then Director of Technology and responsible for the selection of UK Government records for permanent preservation. He also worked as a consultant for UNESCO and was involved with the International Council on Archives. David's current research interests centre around post truth and silences in archives. His recent publications include *The Silence of the Archive* with Val Johnson and Simon Fowler (2017) and with Michael Moss, Overlapping Temporalities – the judge, the historian and the citizen, *Archives* (2017).

Frank Upward worked as an archivist, records manager and information manager before accepting a position at Monash University, Australia, where he designed and taught a wide range of courses. He is best known internationally for his records continuum model and his collaborative work with Sue McKemmish.

Geoffrey Yeo is an Honorary Senior Research Fellow in the Department of Information Studies at University College London (UCL). Before joining UCL in 2000, he worked as an archivist for the Corporation of the City of London, St Bartholomew's Hospital, London, and the Royal College of Physicians of London. He has also worked as a freelance archivist and records manager and as a consultant to the International Records Management Trust. In 2010 he was Visiting Professor at the School of Library, Archival and Information Studies at the University of British Columbia, Vancouver, Canada. He is the editor of *Principles and Practice in Records Management and Archives*, a series of professional texts published by Facet Publishing. His published work won the Society of American Archivists Fellows' Ernst Posner Award in 2009 and the Hugh A. Taylor Prize in 2013.

Introduction

Caroline Brown

It is into the future we go, to-morrow is the eventful thing for us
H. G. Wells, *The Discovery of the Future* (1913, 19)

In his 1902 lecture to the Royal Institution, *The Discovery of the Future*, H. G. Wells argued that the future was knowable. There were, he said, two types of mind: one, common to the majority, which scarcely thinks of the future at all and one which thinks constantly of things to come. For the former 'life is simply to reap the consequences of the past' but for the latter 'life is to prepare for the future' (Wells, 1913, 6). It is not surprising, he believed, that most people look to the past in all its familiarity and relative certainty rather than face the future and wander 'like a lost child in the blankness of things to come' (Wells, 1913, 21). For Wells, however, while our individual fates might not be clear, an inductive knowledge of human destiny is possible and we should 'aspire to, and discover and use' (Wells, 1913, 40) an understanding of our shared future.

Thirty years ago, Hugh A. Taylor, in his article '*Transformation in the Archives: Technological Adjustment or Paradigm Shift?*', echoed this viewpoint (Taylor, 1987). Quoting Raimundo Panikkar ('knowledge is fundamentally the possibility of prevision, of foreseeing the future and thus also of mastering it'), he argued that we should be 'initiating causes to produce certain calculated effects' (Taylor, 1987, 13). Taylor was writing about the impact of the new information society, automation and technology on the archive profession. In some ways his world already seems very different to our own; his statement that 'fifty to 60 per cent of office workers are expected to have microcomputers by the mid-1990s' (Taylor, 1987, 21) reminds us how swift technological change has been. The issues he raises are very familiar though: the impact of different media on culture and society, the preservation of digital records, appraisal, distributed and de-centralised systems, the role of experts, new ways of searching for information, and mediated and unmediated access. His discussion of finding aids and hierarchical archival description remains, thirty years on, refreshing and quietly subversive. Catalogues are dreary, controlling 'snapshots' and users delight in serendipity, which allows them to make discoveries (in spite of archivists), whereas 'the search room of the near future will house not a city of scant entries, but a blizzard of information through which the researcher must find a way' (Taylor, 1987, 22).

Some parallels can be drawn between Wells and Taylor. They were both writing at a time of rapid societal change, for Wells 'this present time is a period of quite extraordinary uncertainty and indecision upon endless questions' (Wells, 1913, 9) and Taylor's world was in the midst of a subsequently much quoted transformational 'paradigm shift'. Both cautioned against looking solely to the past for guidance and sought to explore a vision of the future which could help us understand and influence our actions in the present. The world is, of course, always changing, we stand on shifting sands in our view of the present (and of the past and future) and, if the recordkeeping literature is to be believed, we are still in the throes of our seemingly endless paradigm shift. We should always be looking to things to come to set our current and future direction.

It seems appropriate though, thirty years on from Taylor's article, to pause and consciously revisit the future. Rather than simply rehash discussions which focus on worries about the role of recordkeeping, about our inability to keep up with the digital world or about our need to review and change our principles (or even reinforce and reiterate our principles), this book seeks to follow the example of Hugh Taylor. As Barbara Craig said in her commentary on his article, Taylor, with imagination and insight, went beyond repeating the 'inchoate misgivings most archivists feel in the new age of information overload' (Craig, 1987, 7). The following chapters seek to emulate this and to do what Wells advocated by exploring the future with creativity but also with specificity.

The authors in this volume were given a free rein to examine the present and to imagine the archival future. Many of the topics and issues they have chosen echo those mentioned by Taylor but this should be a source of comfort rather than disquiet. Rather than representing passivity or stagnancy, this surely offers an insight into what the archival profession was and is about: preserving and facilitating access to records (or archives or information) and understanding the impact that this can have on society's memories and actions. However, as archivists we understand contexts, and changing contexts offer new ways of articulating and discussing these issues as well as presenting new insights into the future. This is what this book hopes to do.

In the first chapter, Kate Theimer reflects on the topic that occupied Hugh Taylor: the impact of technology on archives and archivists. She is mostly concerned with the latter and explores whether the world is moving away from professionalism towards standardisation, bypassing gatekeepers and automating professional tasks. Theimer discusses the resulting archival anxiety and the possible impact of these developments on our work and values, and on the relevance of archivists. The conclusions she draws foreshadow those of subsequent authors; she focuses on the importance of 'narrative, storytelling, meaning-making, context providing' (see Chapter 1), on adding a human element to automation and on emphasising the importance of authenticity in order to ensure our relevance in the archival future.

Luciana Duranti offers a wide-ranging exploration of today's world, which she sees as partly characterised by emotive anti-intellectualism and anti-professionalism. Social media has encouraged distributed popularism and misinformation and this has been facilitated and manipulated by large-scale and complex technologies. In this environment, and when information is constantly reused, repurposed and divorced from its original context, where do notions of trust, truth, evidence, integrity and reliability sit? And what is the role of recordkeepers and recordkeeping in all of this? Duranti sees the future as one of a multidisciplinary collaboration of techniques and policies in which a new breed of archivist, or information professional, with an understanding of technology develops tools to help users identify records, evaluate their reliability and trace contexts.

One of the technologies that Duranti discusses is blockchain and this is further explored by Victoria Lemieux. She positions her discussion in the context of what she sees as gradual changes in archival thinking such as a shift from hierarchies towards interconnected relationships. This is reflective of a change in the wider information landscape which is increasingly characterised by globalised, decentralised, autonomous networks. Information, and records, are kept in distributed networks using technologies such as blockchain; control is dispersed overseen by computer scientists and engineers. Lemieux, like Duranti, argues that the role of the archivist remains essential in ensuring that these records remain trustworthy and that the importance of their contextual nature is not ignored.

Archivists have always been responsible for preserving and providing access to evidence. They have always understood that this involves preserving information about context as well as the record itself, and this preservation has always involved selection, a decision about what to keep and what not to keep. Duranti and Lemieux see a continuing role for archivists in championing evidence and context and in the fourth chapter Geoffrey Yeo discusses the position of appraisal in the archival future. Yeo asks what the point of appraisal is: is it to provide better records, to ensure records are easier to find or simply required because space is limited? He explores whether these factors are still relevant in a digital world and whether, in fact, we might reach a stage where we keep everything, which would, after all, ensure a more complete archival record. In a world where tasks are becoming increasingly automated, Yeo suggests increasingly sophisticated methods of retrieval and e-discovery may erode the need for appraisal in its traditional sense. However, there will still be a role for human judgement and archival expertise may revolve around creation, identifying sensitive information or providing selected pathways into the mass of information available.

Jenny Bunn's chapter focuses on archival processing. Rather than simply discussing the difficulties with traditional approaches and suggesting solutions, she revisits some existing discussions. By unpicking these she explores what we mean by processing and whether we need to rearticulate what we do to prepare us for the future. For Bunn, processing might mean importing information from external systems but as archivists we should appreciate that it is more than this; it involves not just metadata but meaning and understanding and the relation between elements. Processing also means describing records as well as documenting a range of entities, relationships and activities, and understanding and articulating this can help us in the digital world. Bunn argues that while technology might allow much of this to be done automatically, there is still a need for the involvement and mediation of archivists, particularly in the realm of sense-making.

E-discovery and the archivist's participation in this is explored by Sonia Ranade using the example of the UK's National Archives where, she explains, the past is now digital and where (in 2017) remote access to digital resources exceeded on-site use by a factor of more than three hundred to one. Ranade's chapter opens up a world of possibilities where technology can help to create a rich, living, useable archive, but one that remains anchored to context and provenance (in all its aspects). At the same time the records that archivists are responsible for are different, they may be messy and changing, and the experience they provide may be as important to capture and access as the information within them. For Ranade, archivists should still play a central role as they understand trust and usability, and they know that discovery involves context and the importance of 'enabling the reader to explore content through the lenses of time, place and identity' (see Chapter 6).

Barbara Reed's chapter takes us away from discoverability and focuses on records and the reasons that they are kept in terms of the rights and representation of users. In this context, Reed and her colleagues discuss recordkeeping informatics that encourages a practical approach to the design of systems and which takes into account issues of evidence, authenticity and accountability. Using the example of children in care, the authors argue that recordkeepers can bring together multiple disciplines and perspectives. By under-standing that records change and are pluralised and operate over time and organizations, recordkeeping professionals can help to ensure that richly representative and authentic records are kept and are easily accessible. The authors argue that recordkeeping informatics is an innovative way of thinking and acting that, by 'addressing the technical, social and knowledge forming aspects of the archive', provides building blocks for our archival future (see Chapter 7).

Reed and her colleagues see the future as an opportunity for a change in perceptions of the role of archivists. In the following chapter,

Michael Moss and David Thomas see the future as a chance to challenge concepts of archives themselves. By arguing that the internet is the archive, they explore questions of what the archive is or has been. The internet allows the past to be in the present where the past and the present are constantly happening; as events are witnessed and re-witnessed, archives are no longer closed and hidden but alive. At the same time the authors explore whether it is possible to 'archive' the internet and where these developments leave an archivist's traditional role as mediator and facilitator of access. In a world where users have direct contact with 'the archive', where nothing is fixed and where temporality loses its meaning, where is the space for archival principles?

This may imply a dilution, at the very least, of the importance of traditional archival ideas. In the final chapter, Craig Gauld, while acknowledging that there has been a 'golden age' of archival ideas, argues that this age has gone. This he sees as reflective of the current environment where big ideas are no longer welcomed, where experts are ridiculed and where fake news is the norm. This post-truth information age has turned users into consumers who are no longer interested in context and whose needs (even archiving needs) are being met by big technology firms who are developing algorithms to do the work that archivists used to do. Gauld's summary of the present might imply that his vision of the archival future is pessimistic, but his conclusion is broadly in line with that of the other authors. Archivists have always and will continue to preserve and provide access to contextualised evidence; whatever the circumstances, this is at the heart of our professional skills and knowledge and forms the basis of our importance to society.

If there is a theme that runs through this volume it is that there is a future for archives and that, despite automation, there are specific skills and knowledge that archivists can, and should, bring to this future. We may worry about our roles, debate the relevance of our standards and actions, and even question what the archive of the future might be, but a look back thirty years to Hugh Taylor's article shows us that there is nothing new in this. The world keeps on turning, archives (however we define them) continue to be created, and if we do not get involved then who will?

Two recent developments demonstrate that archives have not been relegated to an analogue graveyard and that new technologies bring new opportunities and an accompanying recognition of the importance of what we do. In a move which links archives with the building blocks of human life, a Deep Purple recording of *Smoke on the Water* has been stored on DNA and added to the UNESCO Memory of the World programme (Twist Bioscience, 2017). Imagine a future where within us we have not only our individual past and present, our own story in DNA, but alongside that other stories and other archives. At the other end of the spectrum, as Elon Musk is getting ready to go to Mars, space scientists are preparing to hurl an archive of our civilisation into space with a view to communicating with other species over billions of years (Tasoff, 2018). As extraordinary as this project seems, it involves very familiar themes: the selection of information, applying metadata to ensure it can be accessed and understood, providing effective storage and, most importantly, preservation (in this case with the aim of ensuring the preservation of authentic evidence of the human race). In all cases the inference is that these actions will require human as well as computer input.

This scenario may not be the future that most of us will face, but we do face a future and a future that involves archives. This is a future in which our skills are needed but, as the authors in this book show, it is also a future which will require us to be adaptive and to embrace new circumstances and challenges. While this is rather an obvious statement, it is one that bears repeating particularly when combined with a call for a renewed ambition for the profession. H. G. Wells believed that humans should look to the future and should be prepared to alter and adapt according to what they saw there. He had a confidence in the continued, albeit altered, existence of the human race (and beyond), so let us continue to have confidence in the existence, in some form, of the archival profession and a belief in our continued relevance. As Wells said:

All this world is heavy with the promise of greater things, and a day will come, one day in the unending succession of days, when beings, beings who are now latent in our thoughts and hidden in our loins, shall stand upon this earth as one stands upon a footstool, and shall laugh and reach out their hands amid the stars.

(Wells, 1913, 61)

References

Craig, B. L. (1987) Meeting the Future by Returning to the Past: commentary on Hugh Taylor's Transformations, *Archivaria*, **25**, 7–11.

Tasoff, H. (2018) *Putting Civilization in a Box for Space Means Choosing Our Legacy*, www.space.com/39786-send-civilization-to-the-stars.html.

Taylor, H. A. (1987) Transformation in the Archives: technological adjustment or paradigm shift, *Archivaria*, **25**, 12–28.

Twist Bioscience (2017) Iconic Performances of Deep Purple's '*Smoke on the Water*' and Miles Davis' '*Tutu*' Performed at the Montreux Jazz Festival Stored on DNA for the First Time, www.businesswire.com/news/home/20170929005168/en/Twist-Bioscience-Collaborators-Microsoft-University-Washington-Preserve.

Wells, H. G. (1913) *The Discovery of the Future*, B. W. Huebsch.

1

It's the end of the archival profession as we know it, and I feel fine

This chapter is an adapted version of a talk given at the 2016 annual meeting of the Association of Canadian Archivists in Montreal.

Kate Theimer

Introduction

When I was approached to provide a plenary address for the Association of Canadian Archivists' meeting in Montreal, I started out with a vague idea about exploring how technology is contributing to trends in innovation in archives. As a natural result, I've been trying to learn more about how technology and the internet are affecting other professions. I kept thinking that someone must be writing about this and lo and behold I found a book: *The Future of Professions: how technology will transform the work of human experts* by British father and son, Richard and Daniel Susskind. Published in 2016, it was exactly the book I was looking for, and it has changed my own thinking about the future of archives, as well as the main thrust of the talk I was to give. It gave me greater insight into trends I had already observed, what drives innovation and where the roots of the next phase of innovation lie for our profession. It provided evidence for my anecdotal observations and gut feelings, surfaced new ideas and challenged some old ones. It proved to be a great inspiration when writing the talk that provides the basis for this chapter.

My observations here draw heavily from the Susskinds' book, but primarily in form of a remix, slicing and dicing their observations and pulling the ones that best illustrate how their argument applies to the archival profession and how it relates to what we're doing today and will be doing tomorrow. In a nutshell, the Susskinds argue that we are currently in the transitional phase between 'a print-based industrial society' and a 'technology-based Internet society' (Susskind and Susskind, 2016, 151). We can see around us indications of what that technology-based internet society will be like. When it fully arrives, it will be, they claim, radically different and will bring about the end of the professions as we know them today. The professions they focus on in the book are primarily law, medicine, accounting and the like, but their analysis seems applicable to archivists as well. In this chapter I will begin by summarising some of their observations about how the way we work has changed and will change, review some of the current trends they identify, put them in an archival context and address how they can contribute to our own innovation. Following on from this I will address some of the possible reactions to applying their arguments to archives. Finally, I will move up to a higher level and talk briefly about how I think their work can inform our thinking about the future of our profession.

Technology and professionalism

As we travel this road to our new future, the Susskinds claim that the professions will undergo two parallel sets of changes. The first will be dominated by automation. Traditional ways of working will be streamlined and optimised through the application of technology. The second will be dominated by innovation. Increasingly capable systems will transform the work of professionals, giving birth to new ways of sharing practical experience. In the long run this second future will prevail, and our professions will be dismantled incrementally (Susskind and Susskind, 2016, 271.)

The real crux of their argument is the focus on what they call *increasingly capable systems*. They write: 'the leap we ask of readers is to contemplate the impact of Watson-like technology when it is applied across the professions' (Susskind and Susskind, 2016, 165). For 'Watson-like technology' think about advanced artificial intelligence applied pervasively across virtually every aspect of our future lives. Innovation, in their view, 'enables ways of making [professional knowledge] available that simply were not possible (or even imaginable) without the systems in question' (Susskind and Susskind, 2016, 112).

At this point we might consider timeframes. However, the Susskinds explicitly do not discuss this and neither will I as it is impossible to predict with any kind of accuracy the pace of technological change and adoption. Their book – and this chapter – isn't about when something will happen, but rather looking at what we know has happened already and is happening, and thinking about the future, based on those observations. So, with that out of the way, back to my summary of their observations.

Another keystone to the Susskinds' argument is a framework for what they call the *evolution of professional work*. This framework consists of four stages: craft, standardisation, systemisation and externalisation. Externalisation 'is the stage at which the practical expertise of human experts is made available to non-specialists on an online basis' (Susskind and Susskind, 2016, 202). Generally speaking, it's desirable to move each part of your work as far along the framework as possible – or, as they put it: 'our claim is that for any piece of professional work, it is possible to decompose the work into constituent tasks and allocate each task to the most appropriate boxes [craft, standardisation, systemisation, externalisation]' (Susskind and Susskind, 2016, 198). I think we can easily relate to this framework of progress in our own profession – the move from every aspect of our work being a 'bespoke', one-off, handcrafted task, to standardisation in which we developed checklists, reusable forms, standard procedures, etc., to systemisation, in which the work is executed by systems, and to externalisation. As we think about automation and innovation in our field then, we need to actively pursue this process of, as the Susskinds say, *decomposing* our work into tasks and then figuring out how far down the framework we can push each task, realising that there will eventually be very few that truly need to remain in the realm of 'craft', or even perhaps of standardisation.

Another important element of their argument is that:

> There are, in a sense, two new divisions of labor arising in society, both focused on providing alternatives to the traditional professions: the first is a reallocation of effort away from professionals towards different types of people; the second is away from professionals towards a variety of machines.
>
> (Susskind and Susskind, 2016, 215)

Again, this makes sense when you think about the progression of tasks along that framework. As you move from craft to standardisation to systemisation to externalisation, it is increasingly possible to shift the work from experts or professionals to people with less advanced, or different, skills, as well as to machines.

This, then, is the world these authors think will come to dominate us. You might be skeptical that this will ever really come to pass for archives (and I will address this in due course), but I hope that enough of what I have said (and will say) will ring true and that you will, as I did, buy into their essential argument. This is already happening as the following review of some of the trends and patterns the Susskinds identify in their book demonstrates. For each I'll try to explore how their views are applicable to archives and also discuss how we can take advantage of this to push innovation in our own field.

The end of gatekeepers

The first of these trends characterising what, for the Susskinds, may be the end of the professional era is the bypassing of traditional gatekeepers:

> We are already seeing some work being wrested from the hands of traditional professions. Some of the competition is coming from within. We observe professionals from different professions doing each other's work. They even speak of 'eating one another's lunch' . . .. We also see intra-professional friction, when, for example, nurses take on work that used to be exclusive to doctors, or paralegals are engaged to perform tasks that formerly were the province of lawyers. . . . But the competition is also advancing from outside the traditional boundaries of professions—from new people and institutions. . . . Stepping forward are data scientists, process analysts, knowledge engineers, systems engineers, and many more.   (Susskind and Susskind, 2016, 107)

The Susskinds present this as a negative and certainly in many cases it is, but if you approach this from the point of view of what's best for your audiences, collections and budget, there may be value in embracing this trend. Along with asking 'how far along the framework can I push this task?', also ask 'would it be better (or cheaper) for someone else to be doing this task?'

I think we'll also recognise another aspect of this trend, identified by the Susskinds as 'practical expertise being made available by recipients of professional work—in effect, sidestepping the gatekeepers' (Susskind, 2016, 107). Recipients of our professional work? Historians, genealogists, researchers of all kinds, sharing online what they've learned from working in our archives and with our records? That certainly happens too. And again, if our mission is to assist in getting information out there, as professionals we should be supportive of this 'bypassing the gatekeepers' trend and looking for ways to harness it ourselves (as indeed I think the profession has been for some time). Related to this, supporting it and inspiring it, is the way technology and the internet supports the growth of 'do-it-yourself' or DIY or maker culture, enables people to create their own collections and archives of digital and digitised materials, shares them and creates associated communities.

Related to the bypassing of gatekeepers is the trend the Susskinds term *diversification*, which '...involves professionals extending their areas of expertise into new disciplines, often those lying next to the ones over which they already have mastery' (Susskind and Susskind, 2016, 117). Again, we've seen this happen as our historian and librarian colleagues seek to extend their areas of professional activity, if sometimes not the accompanying expertise, into the field of archives. In a corporate setting, diversification may allow clients to rely on only one firm for a suite of related needs – 'one stop shopping', if you will. Again, rather than looking at this only as a negative, as others encroaching on our turf, should we not consider this idea ourselves and examine ways in which we can also extend our areas of expertise into related disciplines? This blurring of professional roles and the elimination of 'bright lines' between professions as people and organizations seek to adjust to a changing playing field is a hallmark of the transition into the end of the professional era.

Proactive professionalism

A second trend the Susskinds identify is a shift from a reactive to a proactive approach to professional work. Again, in their words: 'traditional professional work is reactive in nature. The recipient of the service tends to initiate the engagement and then the professional responds' (Susskind and Susskind, 2016, 107). You get sick, you go and see a doctor. The doctor doesn't call you regularly to ask if you're sick. This sounds very reminiscent of what we might call 'old school' archival work, or that which is done in a more craft-based environment. For me, the way we do reference and reader services comes to mind as an example of how archives have moved from a reactive to a proactive approach. Rather than just waiting for questions to come in, we try to anticipate what people may want to know about and post online resources so that they can help themselves. Another way to think about this shift in terms of how we can innovate as archivists is to look for ways in which people don't know they could benefit from our help until it's too late by reaching out to potential donors and organizational records creators, for example. We have already been innovating by focusing more on upfront commun-ications, outreach, planning, risk management and so on, but we can continue to find ways to make people aware of our services and resources before they even think of looking for them.

Taking this to a more sophisticated level is what the Susskinds refer to as the *embedded knowledge model* in which expert knowledge or rules are embedded in systems and environments so that problems can be avoided before they start. In this model, 'often, indeed, the expertise and its method of delivery will effectively be concealed from those who benefit from its presence' (Susskind and Susskind, 2016, 225). The obvious and perhaps most desirable example of this for our field might be incorporating automated records management into systems and platforms, so that not only would users not need to be conscious of it or execute it, but they also would not be able to circumvent it.

This move from a reactive to a proactive approach to accessing information has had a negative effect on the professions that serve an intermediary function. The example used in the book is travel agents, who were once widely used by many people as intermediaries with hotels, transportation providers and attractions. The ability – and indeed, the preference – of people to interact easily and directly with many kinds of businesses has resulted in the 'disintermediation' of these professionals' roles. The Susskinds observe that 'in response, some innovative professionals are seeking to reintermediate themselves, that is, insert themselves in new places in the supply chain. They are helping in new ways' (Susskind and Susskind, 2016, 121–2).

As intelligent systems are developed that 'disintermediate' archivists from our traditional work, such as those that can serve as intermediaries between people and archival materials, supplying services that generate archival descriptions and answer reference queries (Siri for archives?), another area for potential innovation in our field is to consider where and how we could reintermediate ourselves into the creation, management and use of our holdings? Where else in the information lifecycle could we help in new ways?

Another trend which should resonate with us, I think, is the Susskinds' discussion of how the internet has stimulated 'latent demand' for professional knowledge and services, which is related in some ways to a more proactive approach. Latent demand is when people want or would benefit from information or services, but, in the authors' words, 'to obtain this today in the traditional form is too costly, confusing, and forbidding' (Susskind and Susskind, 2016, 133). Sounds like a perfect description of how some people would view actually visiting a physical archive to access information. Too costly, confusing and forbidding. However, as the Susskinds conclude, when free or low cost online options are available, people use them. For many of us a good example of this is TurboTax, the automated online tax preparation service. We may have wanted professional help doing our taxes, but we didn't want to bother with finding and working with an accountant. However, if that knowledge is embedded in an online system we can use from home, we embrace it. I think this is also exactly what we've seen from putting digital collections online; people use them who would never have sought out archival material before. But to spur further innovations, are there other areas in which we can take advantage of our knowledge and resources to meet latent demand? Pushing out information on 'personal digital archiving' and preserving family, community and organizational records of all kinds seems like another good example, but are there others? What kinds of information do people need or want that we can make easier for them to access?

Communication, participation and data

Although it seems in some ways self-evident, I appreciated that the Susskinds included in their round-up of trends the proliferation of different ways of communicating. For us today this means largely social media and so forth, but the larger point is that embracing new methods needs to become a regular business practice, not an exceptional event. The authors take a minute to pat themselves on the back for recognising before many others did that the use of email would become a standard and accepted form of communication between lawyers and clients. Even though for every Facebook that emerges as a powerhouse, there will be an unknown number of Second Lifes that peter out to virtually nothing, we cannot choose to put our heads in the sand and not explore new ways people work, record their lives, want to communicate with us and access information. With scare resources, it is a delicate balance to know when to jump in, but continually trying out new things and adapting to the changing landscape of communication needs to be a regular part of all our work.

Similarly, the Susskinds note the changes and opportunities wrought by the proliferation of crowdsourcing efforts and widespread online participation – that is, short of using machines, technology allows the use of networks of people, linked by a platform. Again, these people working on a problem may sometimes be professionals, sometimes not. The larger point is that the problems these networked people are able to tackle are the ones that could not have been tackled in the past. Here are just two non-archives examples. As the Susskinds write:

> In 2009 the British Government published online, 700,000 individual documents that related to the expenses of British MPs. In response, the *Guardian* newspaper built an online platform to host these documents, and asked readers collectively to sift through them, a task too large for any one person alone, and flag those that might be of interest, adding analysis if need be. A community of over 20,000 individuals engaged in what was, in effect, a public audit.
>
> (Susskind and Susskind, 2016, 93 footnote)

Another recent example is the Panama Papers, in which journalists from 107 media organizations in 80 countries analysed 11.5 million documents, with the first results being made available in a little more than a year. In both these examples we have people – professionals and non-professionals – carrying out work on a different scale and in a different way than was previously possible. Collaboration – online and in person, with other professionals and the public – will continue to be a means for turning innovative ideas into reality, and the collaborative trend will continue to become more influential in our future.

The next trend not only excites me, but I love the way it was phrased: *mastery of data*. For professions such as law and medicine, the Susskinds talk about this in terms of both gathering and analysing data about their own work and using data sets generated by others. Archivists need to become, if we are not already, masters of data, or to use a less romantic title, data scientists. We need to understand how to apply the tools and techniques of 'big data' to data, both big and small, that we generate in the course of our work and that is a part of our holdings. While certainly not all of us would ever be actually doing the work of creating those tools, or even implementing them, we need to know what is possible and useful so that we can work with others to generate meaningful outputs. The Susskinds note that 'the use of Big Data should identify trends and unearth knowledge that professionals simply had not noted or known of in the past' (Susskind and Susskind, 2016, 163). I suspect that, just as at one point it was acceptable for an archivist to say 'I don't know anything about computers' but today that seems archaic, someday it will seem absurd for an archivist to say 'I don't know anything about data science'.

Innovation and anxiety

We can all recognise trends in the recent history of our profession in these larger trends that the Susskinds have observed affecting professions across the board. While we may think of ourselves as a narrow, specialised (and special) profession, we are just as subject to the enormous shift from 'a print-based industrial society' to a 'technology-based internet society' (Susskind and Susskind, 2016, 151) as the rest of the professions. The value for us in this kind of analysis is the recognition that these trends and shifts are something we need to capitalise on and be a part of rather than try to fight against.

It's worth noting that when we talk about innovation or innovative practices, we are often talking about exactly the kinds of trends the Susskinds highlight – automating, standardising, systemising and externalising – which will result in shifting tasks from professionals to paraprofessionals, related professionals, volunteers, crowdsourcers and increasingly capable machines. In the future, this will also include using the embedded knowledge model, so that tasks are carried out automatically behind the scenes.

The recent history of the profession has also demonstrated innovations arising out of the kinds of changing work patterns the Susskinds discuss, such as efforts to reintermediate ourselves into other parts of the process – identifying where and how we can provide new services and knowledge to capitalise on latent demand, informing the development of these increasingly capable machines, using the tools of data science to understand and help others understand new kinds of data sets and identifying where we can diversify our own profession to take on some of the roles of related professions. We've done some of these more than others, but certainly the current image of an innovative archivist is one who is flexible, data-driven, proactive and not tied to a narrow, constricted view of our professional role.

Now, I must, in all honesty, out myself as having once had, as Richard and Daniel Susskind titled a chapter in their book, 'Objections and Anxieties'. Mine were based on a mélange of the arguments I'm about to review, with a good healthy dose of fear thrown in for good measure. It's reasonable to respond to the vision of the future I've described by saying that either this will never happen in archives or that this should never happen in archives. However, those arguments don't necessarily hold water.

First, this vision of the future clearly assumes that the shift from a print-based (or analogue) society to a digital one has been completed, and yet we know that we will doubtless never reach a point at which all analogue materials have been digitised. These increasingly capable machines will be of little use if information is not in digital form, right? Well, yes, but – and I think we've seen evidence of this as a trend as well – I would argue that in the future that which is not digital will not matter. Of course, it will matter to a select group of people (and it will still have value), just as the cuneiform writing on tablets still has value and matters to a small group of scholars. (Although, even people who need to access the non-digital materials will probably, as they do now, want you to scan it and send copies to them.) The key question isn't will everything be digitised, but rather will we have completed the shift from a print-based *society* to a digital internet one? As the Susskinds observe, right now we're stuck between the two, but I think it's fruitless to argue that such a shift is not an inevitable one.

A second argument, and one that's common across professions, is that 'a machine can't do all the parts of my job'. My assessment of the Susskinds' response to this is that, yes, for the most part, it can. They spend quite a bit of time exploring people's anxiety with this issue, observing:

> There is a deeper level at which professionals will need to revisit their relationship with technology. To insist that machines should, as it were, know their place, namely in the back office and not on the front line, is to ignore the signals of change. Instead two new forms of relationships need to be developed, and each demands new skills and an open mind. The first is the notion that machines and systems will work alongside tomorrow's professionals as partners. The challenge here is to allocate tasks, as between human beings and machines, according to their relative strengths. . . . The second relationship is harder to concede. It is based on frank recognition that some systems will soon be manifestly superior at discharging entire bodies of work that today are undertaken by people – machines, in other words, will replace human beings.
>
> (Susskind and Susskind, 2016, 117)

For many archivists, the idea that a machine would be able to be manifestly superior at reviewing records for personally identifiable information (PII) or potentially restricted information is fine. But when we come to answering reference queries or making appraisal decisions, how willing will we be to trust algorithms? Are these professional tasks not suitable for machines because they require creativity and thought? The Susskinds argue: 'what may appear to be non-routine today may in fact be *routinizable* in the future' (Susskind and Susskind, 2016, 120). And 'just because a professional task is non-routinizable, this does not mean that it cannot be performed by a machine – another theme of this book is that machines can undertake some non-routine tasks *not* by rendering them routine but by tackling them in entirely different ways (for example, using statistics rather than the reasoning that is characteristic of humans)' (Susskind and Susskind, 2016, 120).

However, even if we accept that machines will be able to do many of the tasks of a professional archivist, I'm sure some would make the case that such tools would be beyond the reach and budgets of a lot of archival repositories. These will be the Rolls Royce of systems and most of us will still be on a Ford Fiesta budget. But, again, technology trends argue otherwise. In the not too distant past, many of the gadgets on the original *Star Trek* television series seemed impossible, and yet variants of them exist today. More recently, in the 1987 movie *Wall Street*, when the character played by Michael Douglas (the one who said 'Greed is good') used a cutting edge cell phone at his beach house, it looked like he was holding a brick in his hand. Driverless cars? It's all we hear about, it seems. The examples are endless. The point is, are there archives today that don't have computers or an internet connection? Possibly yes, probably yes. But how relevant are they if we're talking about the profession as a whole? Will all archives be able to carry out their routine functions without professionals? Of course – some do that today, depending on how you define 'an archive'. But, again, we're talking about the profession as a whole, the majority, the professional identity, our consensus of what constitutes a well-run, well-managed archival operation. In the future, I argue, that will include the use of any and all easily available technology, as it does today.

Archival values, archivists and the future

A more compelling argument, perhaps, is not that this won't happen, but that it *shouldn't* happen. That our profession – like all professions – has a tradition and values. That having people involved in certain processes is necessary because the 'human touch' is required. That we shouldn't be entrusting preserving the records of human memory to algorithms. The Susskinds are at their most coldblooded and pragmatic in their response to this kind of defence. They argue that society as a whole and, perhaps most importantly, economic realities don't care about any profession's tradition or values, and people don't value the human touch as much as we might think. What matters is delivering an acceptable level of service as freely and broadly as possible. Having a tailor make a custom suit for a man is a great experience, and I would love to have a specially designed couture gown sewn by talented seamstresses. These are professions with traditions and values, but almost all of us buy our clothes off the rack. If a robot can perform surgery better than a human doctor and I can get an effective diagnosis at three in the morning from an intelligent system, drawing on all the universe of medical knowledge, why wouldn't I choose those options? Some doctors have a truly horrible bedside manner and have no capacity to deliver bad news in a sensitive way. In the future, machines will be able to consistently simulate and fake empathetic human behaviour much more effectively than many human doctors can fake it. Morally, we want to believe we are better off in the hands of our fellow humans, but at times I think we can all admit that's just not the case. More importantly, at what point will those who hold the purse strings stop being willing to pay for it when equivalent or better options are available and at a lower cost?

However, speaking for myself, I don't live in quite as gloomy a world as the Susskinds seem to. I would prefer to talk about the evolution of professions, rather than their end. As beings evolve, they shed characteristics they don't need any more and new ones develop. If it's survival of the fittest professions, I'm invested in making sure archivists survive.

Assuming the basic argument that much of the professional work of archivists will no longer require archivists in the future, what is left for us to take on? How can we continue to provide value that people and organizations will see as unique and worthy of recognition? I'm excited about this evolution because what's left is all the best stuff. What should our profession be focused on as we transition from our current age to the primarily digital future?

Narrative, storytelling, meaning-making, context providing – most of the archivists I know are already great at this and we know that it is what resonates most about archives for many people. Will machines ever be able to do this too? Maybe. Maybe not. But if so, probably not in the same way we would do it. This is pulling materials out of the sea of undifferentiated 'information' and highlighting them, talking about them, connecting them, curating them, telling their story and maybe coming up with platforms and techniques that enable others to do this more effectively too. Do we think about this today as a primary function of archivists, or do we think this should be left to the historians, scholars and museum curators? If the latter, it is important to remember that as we move into the future the lines between the professions will become more blurred. We can bypass gatekeepers too. We can diversify.

Next, outreach and education will be more important than ever. Will there be algorithms that can identify what picture is most likely to attract whatever the future version of Facebook likes will be? Probably, but people will still want to tune into the future equivalent of a podcast to hear someone give a lecture or participate in new opportunities to learn about history, like virtual reality experiences. Remember that the field of education will be just as disrupted as other professions – and there are many good examples of this happening around us now. There will surely be opportunities in this for archives professionals to reintermediate ourselves into education at many levels.

While it might be an uphill battle to keep talking about concepts like authenticity, integrity, reliability, privacy and accountability in the world of the future, I think archivists will and should keep trying. There will be some aspects of the archival tradition that may be even more relevant in our post-textual age.

One new role some may choose to embrace is a historian of obsolete communication forms and practices. They may be specialists in the history of communication and of how bureaucracies and systems worked in 'the past', that is, this textual industrial society in its heyday and waning years. Many of us take our understanding of communication forms for granted and also take for granted that others know or remember what they are and how they work. We often assume people understand forms like old fashioned memos, letters and telegrams. Even email will no doubt come to seem archaic. We can help explain these artefacts and put them in context. We will also, of course, still need to keep identifying new communications platforms and practices and continue to try to figure out how best to use them for outreach, capitalise on latent demand and ensure that their content is appropriately captured for the future.

As we do today, but more so, we will be collaborating with citizen archivists, passionate amateurs and communities of enthusiasts, official community archives and organizational archives, whoever, to help ensure preservation of valuable records, make them accessible and promote their use. Efforts like these are only going to expand, both for digital materials and for gathering up the ephemera of the pre-digital era. The archival world will be more of a true network of repositories of all kinds than it is today. Again, the line between different types of information sources will become more blurred.

Related to this function as a collaborator with people preserving their own materials, as well as education and outreach, will be a continuing need to make people aware of how to preserve their own personal, organizational and family output in an age when almost all of that will be born-digital. In a post-print age, will more advocacy and outreach be necessary to ensure materials are kept? I think so.

In a world with so much digital 'noise', will highlighting archival silences be even more important? Machines and algorithms will be able to identify silences that we may miss, but, with all due respect to our new artificial intelligence (AI) overlords, we as humans will still be able to understand some silences that they will miss and contextualise their findings. We should be working side by side with machines on issues of this kind. For the foreseeable future, I continue to see a role for us in seeking out and ensuring that analogue materials are being digitised and personal recollections are being captured and added to the universe of accessible knowledge. We will still need to keep pursuing the diversification of the digitised record of the past, as well as helping to put that record in context.

Which leads to the area of activism – a topic that deserves to be the subject of its own full-length plenary. Suffice to say that I think our role in documenting the undocumented, surfacing evidence from the past of which people are unaware and doing what we can to advance social justice, wherever possible, will be an important function for archivists moving forward. As Nicola Vernon, a student tweeting for the McGill ACA student chapter, observed: 'it is our duty as archivists to remember what society would prefer to forget' (2016).

These kinds of changes excite me because this shift in our activities would move our focus to some of the most exciting and important things archivists do. In our current environment many of these functions are often regarded as a bonus, an extra, to be done when time permits.

Conclusion

Finally, why does this imaginative journey into one possible – and certainly very viable – future matter? Because in the 'short' term – that is, the foreseeable future – we can work to best take advantage of the conditions as we transition to the digital internet age. We can understand the forces shaping the way people behave and act accordingly. We can try to understand how to best position ourselves, both as custodians of the still present but receding print-based industrial world and as a source of valuable information and expertise in the digital internet society. We can incorporate this understanding into the way we educate and guide the next generations of professionals. This understanding can also inform the way we continue to educate ourselves and the way we talk about our profession to others.

What about the long term? The unforeseeable future? When our transition to the digital internet society is complete? One vision I can see of that future is the evolution of the archival profession into something that has very few connections to what we know today and, in that sense, it will be the end of the profession as we know it. And what might that look like? Maybe some kind of 'Bizzaro Archives World' (Wikipedia, n.d.) in which everything we know is turned on its head. For example:

- The custodial, preservation function of archivists has been handed over to machines, paraprofessionals and rare book and manuscript specialists
- Archivists are valued for being subjective, rather than striving to appear objective
- They identify primarily by area of expertise or research and use archives as a methodology rather than its own area of discipline
- Their primary functions are research, outreach, education and identifying materials to save, digitise and highlight, as well as coordination across collections
- Employment and identification are not tied to physical materials or a physical location. New organizational models enable specialists to work across institutions
- The distinction between museums, libraries and archives may be almost eroded. Archaic analogue books and archival materials are lumped together in the public imagination with museum materials and the people who specialise in them will be analogous to museum curators.

Let's make this more real by looking at a potential example: a person in the future who is expert in, let's say, the history of the documentation of dance. She may be based in association with one traditional collection with strengths in that area, such as the New York

Public Library's Jerome Robbins Dance Division, but she works with dance-related collections across many digital repositories. She generates new scholarship and assists researchers in understanding and accessing resources across digital and analogue repositories. She collaborates with collectors and community archives to preserve analogue and digital materials, promotes and prioritises analogue materials for digitisation, is active on whatever communication platforms exist and works with contemporary dance companies to preserve their documentation.

Notice I'm not calling this person an archivist. At some point along the transition to a digital culture, many in what was once the archival profession decided to rebrand themselves, dropping the title that was so strongly linked to a dusty and irrelevant past. Her title could be something like information historian or meaning maker or memory keeper, or something we can't even imagine yet. Separated from the responsibility of physical custodian of the records, she is free to concentrate on promoting their value and their use and ensuring future records are valued, kept and used as well.

Perhaps I should feel validated that the quote I wanted to use to conclude has already been used. It seems clear that I'm not the only archivist who agrees with the writer William Gibson that 'the future is already here – it's just not very evenly distributed'. Inspired by this vision of a transformed archival profession and my own Generation X roots, I'll turn instead to the words of the band REM and say: 'it's the end of the world as we know it, and I feel fine'.

References

Susskind, R. and Susskind, D. (2016) *The Future of the Professions: how technology will transform the work of human experts*, Oxford University Press.

Vernon, N. (2016) www.twitter.com/mcgill_aca/status/738804186951864320.

Wikipedia (n.d.) https://en.wikipedia.org/wiki/Bizarro_World.

2

Whose truth? Records and archives as evidence in the era of post-truth and disinformation

Luciana Duranti

Introduction

In 2016, the Oxford English Dictionary chose the term 'post-truth' as its Word of the Year, an adjective that it defined as 'relating to or denoting circumstances in which objective facts are less influential in shaping public opinion than appeals to emotion and personal belief' (Oxford English Dictionary, 2016). The term, coined in 1992, has risen in use since the 2016 European Union referendum in the United Kingdom and the United States' presidential election. It relates to a rise of anti-intellectualism that is undermining faith in the professional integrity of all knowledge fields and in the value and authority of records and archives as sources.

Although very 'of the moment', the phenomenon exemplified by the notion of post-truth is not new. Richard Hofstadter's book *Anti-intellectualism in American Life* discusses the phenomenon in 1963 (Lemann, 2014). In addition, intelligence agencies the world over have been using tactics of disinformation – information that is incorrect by design – for decades, as shown by Cobain's narration of the systematic destruction of records perpetrated by the British when leaving their colonies (Cobain, 2016).

A similar phenomenon, identified in 1995 by Robert Proctor, is the deliberate propagation of ignorance. Proctor called its study 'agnotology', from agnosis, the neoclassical Greek word for ignorance or 'not knowing,' and ontology, the branch of metaphysics that deals with the nature of being. Agnotology is the study of wilful acts aimed to spread confusion and deceit (Kenyon, 2016). In the past, these phenomena have been tempered through the mediation exercised by professionals responsible for curating 'the truth' – such as journalists, historians and archivists – which has often, though not always (see Cobain, 2016), succeeded in balancing disinformation and misinformation, or information that is incorrect by mistake, with an accurate revelation of facts.

What has changed in the digital age is the prevalence of a continuous connectivity that lets falsehoods (be they by mistake or by design) circulate at rates unimaginable only a few decades ago. This is combined with the pervasiveness of distribution channels that tend to sidetrack traditional institutions – such as archives, libraries and museums – in favour of a populism where reputation as a trusted source no longer carries much, if any, weight, though a few are calling policy makers to action (Council of Europe, Committee on Culture, Science, Education and Media, 2017).

Challenges

The principle of integrity, common to all knowledge disciplines, demands of professionals a reasonable guarantee of the accuracy, reliability and authenticity of the sources for which they are responsible. However, the phenomena of post-truth and disinformation, though as ancient as time, have been so highly politicised that reliance on sources seems hopelessly mired in partisanship (Despres, 2016), while it becomes increasingly unclear who is responsible for the truthfulness of news stories, marketing and profiling. One might ask: what is the meaning and value of 'truth' at a time when, according to the Pew Research Center for Journalism and Media, 62% of American adults obtain information from social media (Gottfried and Shearer, 2016)?

We know that what people read on social media is filtered: the stories reinforce members' beliefs and those of their friends. After all, these stories are selected by algorithms that make the most money for corporations like Facebook, which operates a network of 79% of online American users (Greenwood, Perrin and Duggan, 2016):

On Facebook, what you click on, what you share with your 'friends' shapes your profile, preferences, affinities, political opinions and your vision of the world. The last thing Facebook wants is to contradict you in any way. The sanction would be immediate: you'd click/share much less; even worse, you might cut your session short. Therefore, Facebook has no choice but keeping you in the warm comfort of the cosy environment you created click after click. In the United States, Facebook does this for 40 minutes per user and per day.

(Filloux, 2016)

The result is a sort of dystopian social realisation of Thomas Kuhn's observation that the nature of scientific fact is not solely based on objective criteria but shaped by the opinions of a community (Kuhn, 2000).

A related, frightening picture emerges when considering personal data. After 9/11, two things that happened in parallel facilitated the gathering of huge amounts of personal data to benefit the business models of certain corporations, simultaneously enabling government surveillance: (1) the ability and practice of private companies to gather personal data; and (2) governments enacting laws demanding access to any and all data (new or old) held by corporations. But the very protection of that private data, which is an individual right, makes it impossible for end users or society as a whole to reach conclusions about the authenticity or provenance of a particular claim, news story or record: the information that could be used to trace them to their sources is protected as private. The whole business model is based on an activity that is fundamentally predatory, since it repurposes other peoples' productive content in a way that makes users the maximum amount of money and encourages unproductive, socially damaging activity, with no reference to the common good, however that is defined (Hoback, 2013).

At the same time, records – their creation, maintenance and preservation – are falling victim to politicians and administrators who fear being held accountable for their actions. In her report 'Access Denied', the then British Columbia Information and Privacy Commissioner, Elizabeth Denham, noted how the practices of documenting actions and decisions, as well as those related to retention and disposition of government records, have been lacking in many respects

(Denham, 2015). This has prompted Denham and other information commissioners to call for a 'duty to document' (Office of the Information Commissioner of Canada, 2016). Yet, detractors claim that recording official facts and acts has a chilling effect on policy deliberations which would become much slower and less decisive (Blair, 2010; Fukuyama, 2014).

Contributing to the above situation, the technical infrastructures that gather and store data have become increasingly complex, often invisible and hidden (Orlikowski, 2007). Records professionals are at a loss to capture much, if any, provenance data about the information found in these infrastructures and, often, even to understand their scope and scale, as well as who controls them. Individuals have no idea which systems are 'hoovering up' their data, or how to prevent them. This is a variation of Peter Steiner's cartoon 'On the Internet, nobody knows you are a dog' (Steiner, 1993), but with nightmarish consequences. Some groups and individuals feel a sense of injustice and are fighting back. They are protesting through the use of hacktivism (Thompson, 2013), and they are using encryption and decentralised information processing technologies, such as the blockchain (Underwood, 2016), to protect the 'truth' (The Syrian Archive, 2016) and their privacy. But can these technologies be trusted?

Trust in technology

Trust is defined by the InterPARES Trust project as the 'confidence of one party in another, based on alignment of value systems with respect to specific actions or benefits, and involving a relationship of voluntary vulnerability, dependence, and reliance, based on risk assessment' (InterPARES Trust, 2017).

Traditionally, trust has been placed in a third neutral party, usually an institution that has no stake in the content of the sources that it preserves. However, as mentioned earlier, these institutions have been sidetracked by the internet and technologies like blockchain are increasingly taking up their authenticating function.

Victoria Lemieux states that although there is not an internationally agreed upon definition of blockchain, it is often described as 'an open-source technology that supports trusted, immutable records of transactions stored in publicly accessible, decentralised, distributed, automated ledgers' (Lemieux, 2017). Blockchain technology is mostly used for land records, financial records and health records. The types of records most frequently found on blockchain are smart contracts and smart trust and estate. Much research is currently being conducted on the use of blockchain to ensure and verify the authenticity of records through time. It is already clear that the hype that surrounds this technology is not going to withstand close scrutiny for a variety of reasons, starting with the fact that the law tends to be location and domain specific while blockchain technology is transjurisdictional and transdomain, and ending with the fact that, as records on blockchain are detached from their administrative, provenancial, procedural and documentary context, while their digital integrity can be proven, their contextual identity and meaning cannot, thus they are unable to be trustworthy sources of facts and acts (Lemieux, 2016).

What is being done?

Third parties have begun to document facts and actions as they happen, but without access to the original sources – as in the case of the Internet Archive's new Donald Trump Archive, consisting of more than 700 'televised speeches, interviews, debates, and other news broadcasts related to… Donald Trump' (Leetaru, 2017). While this new project of the Internet Archive aims to create a historical record, it does so to enable re-use and repurposing of materials shown in broadcasts without the ability to trace the information back to the records held by news agencies, government offices and the Republican and Trump campaigns. As a consequence, the material sits out of its original contexts, providing few means to determine its authenticity or the accuracy and reliability of the facts it presents: news clips taken from a variety of broadcasts and their interpretation by visualisation experts, together with the Trump twitter archives, become 'the record' of the Trump campaign.

Given these circumstances, one wonders where the 'truth' lies, whose version of historical 'facts' will prevail and what role, if any, records and archives as sources will play. While providing information and evidence of facts and acts, records and archives form the infrastructure through which beliefs and values (whether universal, human, cultural, social, personal, political, economic or ethical) are upheld and understood and human institutions structured (Giddens, 1984). The InterPARES Trust research partnership, funded from 2013 to 2018 by a Social Sciences and Humanities Research Council of Canada's Partnership Grant, has developed guidance for strengthening records and archives stored on the internet so that their availability, accessibility and authenticity, as well as the reliability of their content, can withstand attempts to tamper with them and pass any scrutiny about their integrity even in the context of the commercial cloud (InterPARES Trust, 2018). The project has developed a model for Preservation as a Service for Trust (PaaST) and is collaborating with the Object Management Group to make it an international standard (Duranti et al., 2016; Duranti, 2016).

However, how useful is it to have trustworthy records and archives systems if records of actions and decisions are not generated; if those that are created are quickly destroyed as transitory records before entering such systems so that freedom of information can be evaded; if the content of the records that are made or received and properly maintained is selectively taken and used out of context; if claims, news and collected clips are neither traced nor traceable to authoritative documentary sources; and if users of data and information disseminated by broadcasts and social media do not know how to verify their sources and thus lose interest in doing so?

What should be done?

We certainly must establish first whether the traditional role(s) of records and archives professionals in ensuring the contextual accuracy, reliability and authenticity of digital records, irrespective of user, use, reuse and purpose of use, need to be re-examined in order to counter human deception and its amplification on the internet. Are there technical and procedural ways to handle records so that misuse can be more easily identified (Duranti and Rogers, 2011; Bass, 2013)?

Some claim that records and archives professionals should develop and promote a Computational Archival Science (CAS). This is defined as:

An interdisciplinary field concerned with the application of computational methods and resources to large-scale records/archives processing, analysis, storage, long-term preservation, and access, with aim of improving efficiency, productivity and precision in support of appraisal, arrangement and description, preservation and access decisions, and engaging and undertaking research with archival material.

(Computational Archival Science Portal)

The key components of CAS related to reliability will result from making specific changes to existing practices for describing records to help users to better judge their authenticity and the truth value of a particular claim or set of claims that rely upon on it (Bak, 2012; Yeo, 2016).They will also result from a resolution of the argument over whether archivists should promote social justice and social cohesion (Jimerson, 2007; Caswell and Cifor, 2016) or hold on to their traditional claims or goals of objectivity and impartiality by acquiring recorded misinformation as part of the cultural heritage of a society (Hohmann, 2016). Other components would directly address issues of acquisition and preservation, such as the archiving of websites with largely unstructured and widely divergent content, petabyte-level scale, un(der)developed research platforms and diverse creator types.

However, such an undertaking may take years. In the meantime, records and archives professionals should identify the capabilities of existing technological tools (for example, e-discovery, machine-learning tools and visual analytics tools) and easy-to-develop tools in the assessment of records' evidential capacity, traceability of data to their record sources and evaluation of the reliability and authenticity of donated materials, and recommend their use in the design and management of records systems. There are tools that can analyse large volumes of data from various sources and compare and detect patterns in reporting, characterising or recasting information over time and across various sources and geographical locations. There are also tools that link the emerging information patterns to digital records and archives as sources. Records professionals should learn to use technologies like those supporting computational trust, deep-learning, blockchain, smart contracts, and so on, as these can contribute to the accountability and transparency of a decision-making process based on algorithms to ensure a 'digital truth' that leads to fair, ethical and better decisions (Christians and Traber, 1997).

This would also enable records and archives professionals to suggest to government policy makers and legal advisers ways of dealing with the Internet of Things platforms using digital records and archives as sources of evidence. Of course, in order to act as advisors, it is not sufficient for professionals to acquire familiarity with these technologies. They must make sense of the complementary and conflicting aspects of data protection and privacy legislation, the right to be forgotten, transparency, accountability, freedom of information and open public data in light of manipulation of information (for example, for purposes of profiling). As policy makers consider building a new legal framework for algorithmic decision making (such as artificial intelligence), records professionals should think about what guidelines can be defined and promulgated for codifying the requirement for transparency regarding automated decision processes (Association of Computing Machinery US Public Policy Council, 2017).

Yet, none of the above will work if we do not first gain an understanding of the way in which individual identity within different socio-political environments participates in the use or rejection of different sources of evidence in establishing the 'truth'. It is essential to understand whether there are global values that dictate the acceptance or rejection of sources of evidence (Schaeffer, 1992) and how records and archives compare with other memory traditions in terms of their effectiveness in revealing and evaluating power dynamics and establishing the truth within specific socio-cultural configurations.

Sometimes the differences in the way people evaluate sources of evidence are based on the medium/form (packaging) of the sources themselves rather than on the socio-political environment of different communities, populations or professions (Frogner, 2010; Frogner, 2015). Certainly, it is important to develop models for handling different kinds of sources of truth, fostering a meta-literacy that would take people beyond digital literacy (i.e. knowing how to search and find information) to understanding how to evaluate and assess sources of evidence (Mackey and Jacobson, 2016), such as scientific data, which need to be better communicated to and understood by the public (LeVeque, Mitchell and Stodden, 2012; FitzJohn et al., 2014).

Conclusion

It is vital for the survival of democratic societies to promote and support a determined effort by governments, the media and the public to store, provide access to and/or use as verifiable evidence the records and archives residing in trustworthy systems designed according to professionally established requirements. This would enable citizens to trace claims, news and information affecting their lives to such sources and will guide records, archives and media professionals in ensuring the proper contextualisation of all data. There are several actions that could be undertaken to establish digital records and archives as the most accurate, reliable and authentic sources of evidence for the media and the public. In a recent speech, Elizabeth Denham, in her role of Information Commissioner for the United Kingdom, stated that:

> ... information held in WhatsApp accounts, is subject to the FOIA if ... relates to the official business of [a] public body. This includes messages by government officials, advisors, or ministers.... in the context of information rights, it's the message, not the medium that matters.... Use of private email accounts and instant messaging to conduct government business can frustrate good governance and undermine the public's right to know. I see the job of the ICO not only to administer access to information legislation, but to help make sure proper records exist in the first place. (Denham, 2017)

This statement raises the questions: 'what is a proper record in the context we are living now?' and 'exist where'?

In an opinion piece in *Deep Code*, Greenhall (2017) writes: 'we are right in the middle of an existential conflict between two entirely different and incompatible ways of forming "collective intelligence"'. What he is referring to is the attempt by new political and cultural forces to undermine the traditional centralised system relying on a stable hierarchical infrastructure controlling communications (for example, large newspapers, networks and information systems) by bypassing it, destroying it and replacing it with a different system that is decentralised and 'structurally incompatible' with the existing one, because it is fast, idiosyncratic, asynchronous and bottom-up. Greenhall believes that this new system's 'ability to read-plan-react (their "OODA loop") is simply of a higher order than the legacy power structures' (Greenhall, 2017). While social media and android applications are still controlled by these legacy power structures, it is very likely that they will choose to be part of the decentralised system in order to remain in power.

If Greenhall's analysis is correct, the implication is that the will power of established legacy structures such as national Information Commissioners will not have a chance of success. Proper records will not be created even if a duty to document is legislated and what information is generated, in whatever form, will exist out of the control of any established authority. This is an apocalyptic scenario and one that does not include in the equation the records and archives profession.

The profession is well aware of the dangers presented by this era of post-truth and disinformation and is already working at international level with providers of technology and services and network communications, and experts in computer engineering, cyber-security, e-business, e-discovery, digital forensics, evidence law, intellectual rights, investigative reporting, media credibility, journalism, knowledge organization, political science, philosophy and sentiment analysis. Together they are all collaborating in the production of requirements, tools and methods, as well as shared guidelines, to ensure people's ability to access, if not the truth, complete factual information based on authentic, accurate and reliable sources in context.

If this multidisciplinary and international collaboration focuses on the steps necessary to move forward, as outlined earlier, the probabilities of success will be high, resulting in effective records and archives systems controlled by experts in computational archival science and accessed by users whose meta-literacy allows for a thorough understanding of primary sources of evidence, records and archives.

References

Association of Computing Machinery US Public Policy Council (2017) *Statement on Algorithmic Transparency and Accountability*, www.acm.org/binaries/content/assets/public-policy/2017_usacm_statement_ algorithms.pdf.

Bak, G. (2012) Continuous Classification: capturing dynamic relationships among information resources, *Archival Science*, **12** (3), 287–318.

Bass, J. (2013) A PIM Perspective: leveraging personal information management research in the archiving of personal digital records, *Archivaria*, **75**, 49–76.

Blair, T. (2010) *My Political Life*, Hutchinson.

Caswell, M. and Cifor, M. (2016) From Human Rights to Feminist Ethics: radical empathy in the archives, *Archivaria*, **81**, 23–43.

Christians, C. G. and Traber, M. (eds) (1997) *Communication Ethics and Universal Values*, SAGE Publications.

Cobain, I. (2016) *The History Thieves: secrets, lies and the shaping of a modern nation*, Portobello Books Ltd.

Computational Archival Science (CAS) Portal (n.d.) What is Computational Archival Science (CAS)? An Initial Working Definition, http://dcicblog.umd.edu/cas/cas/.

Council of Europe, Committee on Culture, Science, Education and Media (2017) *Online Media and Journalism: challenges and accountability*, Report to the Parliamentary Assembly, Doc. 14228, www.bit.ly/2jQOtWm.

Denham, E. (2015) *Access Denied: record retention and disposal practices of the Government of British Columbia*, Investigative Report F15-3, British Columbia: Office of the Information and Privacy Commissioner.

Denham, E. (2017) The Extent of our Care: archives, memory and information rights, www.ico.org.uk/about-the-ico/news-and-events/news-and-blogs/2017/01/the-extent-of-our-care-archives-memory-and-information-rights/.

Despres, G. (2016) Fact Denial and the Record Under Threat, *Brandeis Records Manager Blog*, December 21, https://blogs.brandeis.edu/records/2016/12/21/fact-denial-and-the-record-under-threat/.

Duranti, L. (2016) Building a Trustworthy System: what will trustworthy systems look like in the future? In Bantin, P. C. (ed.) *Trustworthy Systems for Digital Objects: theory and practice*, 336–50, Rowman & Littlefield Publishers.

Duranti, L. and Rogers, C. (2011) Educating for Trust, *Archival Science*, **11** (3–4), 373–90.

Duranti, L., Adam, J., Giovanni, M., Mumma, C. C., Prescott, D., Rogers, C. and Thibodeau, K. (2016) Preservation as a Service for Trust (PaaST). In Vacca, J. (ed.) *Security in the Private Cloud*, 47–72, CRC Press.

Filloux, F. (2016) Facebook's Walled Wonderland is Inherently Incompatible with News, *Monday Note*, December 4, www.mondaynote.com/facebooks-walled-wonderland-is-inherently-incompatible-with-news-media-b145e2d0078c.

FitzJohn, R., Pennel, M., Zanne, A. and Corwell, W. (2014) Reproducible Research is Still a Challenge, *ROpenSci*, June 4, www.ropensci.org/blog/2014/06/09/reproducibility.

Frogner, R. (2010) 'Innocent Legal Fictions': archival convention and the *North Saanich Treaty* of 1852, *Archivaria*, **70** (70), https://archivaria.ca/index.php/archivaria/article/view/13295.

Frogner, R. (2015) 'Lord, Save Us from the Et Cetera of the Notary': archival appraisal, local custom, and colonial law', *Archivaria*, **79** (Spring), 121–58.

Fukuyama, F. (2014) *Political Order and Political Decay: from the Industrial Revolution to the globalization of democracy*, Farrar, Straus and Giroux.

Giddens, A. (1984) *The Constitution of Society: outline of the theory of structuration*, University of California Press.

Gottfried, J. and Shearer, E. (2016) News Use Across Social Media Platforms 2016, *Pew Research Center: Journalism and Media*, May 26, www.journalism.org/2016/05/26/news-use-across-social-media-platforms-2016.

Greenhall, J. (2017) Situational Assessment 2017: Trump Edition, *Deep Code*, January 25, www.medium.com/deep-code/situational-assessment-2017-trump-edition-d189d24fc046#.ln38etiha.

Greenwood, S., Perrin, A. and Duggan, M. (2016) Social Media Update 2016, *Pew Research Center: Internet & Technology*, November 11, www.pewinternet.org/2016/11/11/social-media-update-2016.

Hoback, C. (2013) *Terms and Conditions May Apply*, documentary film.

Hohmann, P. (2016) On Impartiality and Interrelatedness: reactions to Jenkinsonian appraisal in the twentieth century, *American Archivist*, **79** (1), 14–25.

InterPARES Trust (2013–2018) www.interparestrust.org, http://arstweb.clayton.edu/interlex/en/term.php?term=trust.

Jimerson, R. (2007) Archives for All: professional responsibility and social justice, *American Archivist*, **70** (2), 252–81.

Kenyon, G. (2016) The Man Who Studies the Spread of Ignorance, BBC, January 6, www.bbc.com/future/story/20160105-the-man-who-studies-the-spread-of-ignorance.

Kuhn, T. S. (2000) *The Structure of Scientific Revolutions*, University of Chicago Press.

Leetaru, K. (2017) 'What Data-Mining TV's Political Coverage Tells US', *Real Clear Politics*. https://www.realclearpolitics.com/articles/2017/08/10/what_data-mining_tvs_political_coverage_tells_us.html.

Lemann, N. (2014) The Tea Party is Timeless: Richard Hofstadter's *Anti-Intellectualism in American Life* reviewed, *Columbia Journalism Review*, Sept–Oct., www.cjr.org/second_read/richard_hofstadter_tea_party.php.

Lemieux, V. (2016) Blockchain for Recordkeeping: help or hype? A technical report, DOI: 10.13140/RG.2.2.28447.56488, www.interparestrust.org/trust/research_dissemination.

Lemieux, V. (2017) Blockchain and Distributed Ledgers as Trusted Recordkeeping Systems: an archival theoretic evaluation framework, paper presented at the *Future Technologies Conference* (FTC).

LeVeque, R. J., Mitchell, I. M. and Stodden, V. (2012) Reproducible Research for Scientific Computing: tools and strategies for changing the culture, *Computing in Science and Engineering*, **14** (4), 13.

Mackey, T. P. and Jacobson, T. (2016) How Can We Learn to Reject Fake News in the Digital World?, *The Conversation*, December 6, www.theconversation.com/how-can-we-learn-to-reject-fake-news-in-the-digital-world-69706.

Office of the Information Commissioner of Canada (2016) Backgrounder on a Duty to Document, www.oic-ci.gc.ca/eng/communique-de-presse-news-releases-2016_4.aspx.

Orlikowski, W. J. (2007) Sociometric Practices: exploring technology at work, *Organization Studies*, **28** (9), 1435–48.

Oxford English Dictionary (2016) Word of the Year 2016 is . . ., https://en.oxforddictionaries.com/word-of-the-year/word-of-the-year-2016.

Schaeffer, R. (1992) Transcendent Concepts: power, appraisal, and the archivist as social outcast, *American Archivist*, **5**, 608–19.

Steiner, P. (1993) On the Internet Nobody Knows You're a Dog, *The New Yorker*, July 5.

The Syrian Archive (2016) www.syrianarchive.org.

Thompson, C. (2013) Hacktivism: civil disobedience or cyber crime?, *ProPublica*, January 18, www.propublica.org/article/hacktivism-civil-disobedience-or-cyber-crime.

Underwood, S. (2016) Blockchain Beyond Bitcoin, *Communications of the ACM*, **59** (11), 5–17.

Yeo, G. (2016) Contexts, Original Orders, and Item-Level Orientation: responding creatively to users' needs and technological change, *Journal of Archival Organization*, **12** (3–4), 170–85.

3

The future of archives as networked, decentralised, autonomous and global

Victoria Lemieux

Introduction

There are moments in history – sometimes disruptive instances, but often gradual – when humanity sheds one organizing principle for another. These shifts recursively represent and construct new mental models and major changes in the social and material world around us. In the archival world, for example, we have seen a recent shift away from favouring representation of archival *fonds* in terms of hierarchies towards favouring a view of the *fonds* as networks of interconnected relationships. This paradigm shift within archival descriptive practice is indicative of a larger shift in human schemas of thought and the social and material world – the shift to networks.

Networks are now everywhere. We are seemingly surrounded by them, even enmeshed in them. In a prescient analysis of the rise of networks, Manuel Castells (1996, 5) observes that social development and technological innovation go hand in hand, 'since technology is society and society cannot be understood or represented without its technological tools'. Networks are decentralised – or at least leave the impression of being so; unlike hierarchies, there is no command and control from the top. They represent a completely different sort of organizing principle – of thought ('hive mentality'), of social action (literally, 'social networks') and of our material world (the internet).

Castells (1996, 171) further observes, in relation to the network enterprise, that it is 'that specific form of enterprise whose system of means is constituted by the intersection of autonomous systems of goals'. Thus, not only decentralisation, but autonomy – in the sense of operating (seemingly) without human will or intervention – emerge as defining features of the network organizing principle. Finally, the network *modus operandi* is one that transcends the national or the particular while at the same time encompassing it. It is – or seeks to be – inherently globally interconnected.

Whether the impetus for the 'network shift' has arisen from the material technological world, with, for example, the invention of the internet and the world wide web, or it emerged first as a schema of thought that conjured up the socio-material, or through a dialogic process between the material and the social, is a question that will not be discussed further in this chapter. Instead, this chapter focuses on a relatively recent manifestation of the shift towards the network as organizing principle, which now finds expression in a technological innovation in recording and storing information called *blockchain* technology, and what this means for records and archives in the next 30 to 40 years.

What is blockchain technology?

What is blockchain technology? That question is not easily answered as there is, as yet, no internationally accepted definition (Walch, 2017). Currently, the definition of blockchain technology is as fluid a thing as the informational flows that define the age of networks. Nevertheless, blockchain technology exhibits all the characteristics of the new network operating principle. It is decentralised: many individual nodes operating together to form a peer-to-peer network that records and secures transactions (Narayanan et al., 2016, 27, 51). This is why blockchain technology is often described as a 'distributed ledger' (Pearce-Moses, 2017). Rather than centralising records of account in a book or single computer system, as in the case of a traditional ledger, blockchains distribute copies of records on 'nodes' on a network. The nodes that operate as part of this decentralised network, in theory, are unlimited in number and can operate from any location (Narayanan et al., 2016, 27–8). Thus, at least in the case of public blockchains, blockchain technology exhibits the inherent tendency to globalisation typical of all networks. Each node usually retains a complete copy of the ledger, though some nodes retain only a partial copy of it, that is, 'light nodes' (Narayanan et al., 2016, 71).

As is typical of the network operating model – there is no one in charge of the blockchain per se. Nodes operate in an autonomous manner – again, like all networks – to fulfil a common purpose: the keeping of the ledger (Narayanan et al., 2016, 27–8).

The ledger consists of a series of blocks, within which are transaction records. Transaction records, as the name implies, represent a series of actions that result in changes from one state to another (Narayanan et al., 2016, 51–2). They are created by taking input information of any nature and size and digitally signing it to produce a 256-bit random number known as a hash (Narayanan et al., 2016, 65). This hash is added together to form a block of a certain size. When the block reaches its maximum size, it is chained together with previous blocks by means of a computational 'consensus algorithm' designed to ensure that updates to the ledger are agreed and communicated across the entire network, and that any changes to what has been written to the ledger will be detectable (Narayanan et al., 2016, 28–9). Once written to the network, these transaction records are meant to be immutable (Narayanan et al., 2016, 51).

The hash of the previous block is added to the hashes of the transactions in a new block to produce a new hash, and this hash is subsequently added to the transaction hashes of the succeeding block to produce another new hash, with each block validated using a consensus algorithm. The process repeats to produce a long chain of blocks, hence the name blockchain.

Since the technology is so new and still evolving, there are non-trivial variations in how it operates. Different blockchain platforms use different approaches to validating transactions, such as Proof of Work, Proof of Burn, Proof of Activity, etc. (Briscoe, 2017). Even among blockchain platforms that use the same consensus algorithm, there are variations that make an enormous difference in the behaviour of the network (compare the way that the Proof of Work consensus mechanism performs in the Bitcoin blockchain versus in the Ethereum blockchain, for example (Rosic, 2016)). Some blockchains are public – allowing anyone to join as a node on the network – and others are private, permissioned blockchains which restrict who can join (compare the Bitcoin public blockchain with the Medicchain blockchain, https://medichain.online/#About-MediChain, for example).

Even though one of the basic operating principles of blockchain technology is decentralisation, governance of some blockchains falls under the central control of a single organization or consortium, e.g. the R3C consortium (www.r3.com). Although blockchain technology is closely associated with cryptocurrency, some do not rely upon the use of a token or coin to operate, e.g. Hyperledger (www.hyperledger. org). All these differences make it very challenging to arrive at a standard definition or reference architecture for blockchain technology.

Another reason for the difficulty in devising standards for blockchain technology is that it is not really a single technology at all, but rather an amalgam of several different innovations that have evolved over time (Clark, 2016). These elements came together in what might be called the first blockchain 'use case' – Bitcoin – in 2008. The origins of Bitcoin are shrouded in mystery. Its first public mention was a paper pseudonymously authored by Satashi Nakamoto (2008), whose true identity remains unknown to this day. The Bitcoin blockchain facilitates payments across a decentralised network. These payments are denominated in Bitcoin, a type of 'cryptocurrency', which is not really a coin at all. Rather, it is a representation of an amount of value.

When Bitcoin payments are made from one wallet to another, no movement of actual or virtual coins takes place. Instead, information is transmitted to nodes on the peer-to-peer network. Once mined or validated by means of the Proof of Work consensus mechanism, each node receives an update to the copy of the ledger that it stores which reflects that a certain amount of value in Bitcoin has been deducted from the value attributed to one wallet and added to the value attributed to another wallet (Nakamoto, 2008). Bitcoin wallets hold addresses on the network. These addresses function somewhat like a postal code indicating the destination of a particular transfer of value (Narayanan et al., 2016, 77).

For each public key there is a matched private key. The person who holds the private key controls the wallet (Narayanan et al., 2016, 77). When individuals want to transfer value to someone else's wallet, they must use their private key to digitally sign the transaction. Since there is nothing inherent in the operation of the Bitcoin blockchain that links a person's real world identity to their public-private key pairs, the Bitcoin network is said to operate pseudonymously (Narayanan et al., 2016, 138–44). This has made it popular with those involved in criminal activities who wish to make and receive payments without detection. The association with criminal activity has led many to eschew the use of Bitcoin and its underlying technological structure – blockchain (Lemieux, 2016).

It is important to emphasise that Bitcoin is just one of many use cases, or applications, of blockchain technology. It is tempting to think of blockchain, and even the specific implementation of blockchain which is known as Bitcoin, only in relation to cryptocurrency because of the references to coins and wallets redolent of descriptions of how blockchain technology operates. Now, however, interest in, and use of, both Bitcoin and blockchain technology for other applications is growing rapidly – including for recordkeeping (Lemieux, 2016). In many cases, designers of these solutions are unfamiliar with recordkeeping or digital preservation requirements, and, as a result, whitepapers and marketing literature for these solutions are full of unverified, possibly false, claims (Lemieux, 2016).

Why is blockchain of interest to archives and records professionals?

Any technology that purports to produce immutable records of transactions is of interest to records and archives professionals. This is the stuff of which archives are made. Blockchain technology is already transforming the face of records creation and keeping, just as technological innovations have done before. These changes are occurring in every domain: the recording of civil registrations, real estate transaction recording, medical recordkeeping, the keeping of academic records and beyond (Lemieux, 2016).

In Estonia, for example, blockchain technology is being used for keeping medical records. Records from the Estonian e-Health database that document visits to a doctor, surgery, analysis in a lab and other medical procedures are being hashed and recorded in the Guardtime Keyless Signature Infrastructure (KSI) to protect the integrity of the records (Records in the Chain Project, 2017).

Records from the real estate registry office in the municipality of

Pelotas, Brazil, are being anchored in the Ubitquity blockchain solution in much the same way as in the Estonian e-health solution. In the case of the Brazilian blockchain pilot, however, the components of the blockchain solution are globally distributed with front end elements served from the US and an Israeli-based middleware component, all leveraging a globally distributed Bitcoin network (Lemieux, 2017, 16).

Although these pilots operate as cryptographically secured and decentralised pseudo-mirrors of existing recordkeeping systems, other solutions are already natively generating records on the blockchain. In the Swedish land registry's pilot blockchain system, for example, a 'smart contract' (Szabo, 1997) – essentially, a set of conditional scripts that manage network calls and allow automatic triggering of transactions and permissions – is producing real estate transaction records using a permissioned technical ecosystem which combines enterprise databases with private, permissioned blockchains (Snäll, 2017).

Where once the reliability of records was aided by physically signing and dating documents, registering them and placing them in proximity to one another within a file folder, in a blockchain environment, the signatures are digital, dates are replaced with computer-generated timestamps, registration is transformed into cryptographic hashing and physical proximity of records becomes linked transactions, chained together into blocks over a decentralised network.

This decentralised, often autonomously operating, and, potentially, globally distributed approach to records creation and keeping requires that archives and records professionals learn how to translate existing theories and principles for application into new blockchain recordkeeping environments, even as they have only begun to come to grips with cloud technology. It also requires that they develop a new understanding of how well blockchain-based records creation, management and preservation adhere to records management and archival requirements for the production and preservation of trustworthy records. What does it take to produce accurate, reliable and authentic records using blockchain technology? At this point in time, archives and records professionals are only beginning to wonder about this.

How might blockchain change archival institutions and archival practice?

Just as records creation and keeping is being transformed by the emergence of blockchain technology, there are early signs that these changes, in turn, will transform traditional archival practice. Some of these changes will be incremental and some look set to be much more radical in nature and even use the benefits of blockchain to solve recordkeeping issues. As an example, an InterPARES research team is exploring the possibility of using blockchain technology to address the issue of expiring digital signatures in archives (The TRUSTER Preservation Model (EU31)). The team is working on a solution that they are calling TrustChain, which will anchor hashes of digitally signed documents in a blockchain as a means of ensuring that the authenticity of records transferred to archives is not lost when digital signature certificates expire.

TrustChain proposes to solve a very immediate, practical problem using blockchain technology without radical change to existing archival practice, but will blockchain technology result in fundamental change to archives administration and digital preservation practice? It is difficult to envision how archival institutions, which traditionally have had very centralised operating models and modes of digital preservation, can withstand unchanged the rising tide of networks, decentralisation, autonomy and globalisation. Blockchain technology is disrupting other centralised organizations with its distributed model of trust (Seidel, 2017), so the question arises as to how it would even be possible to preserve a decentralised blockchain network in today's centralised trusted digital repository? The very nature of blockchain technology requires preservation of the mechanism by which decentralised nodes on the network interact. This is not a capability that today's approaches to digital preservation are designed to address.

Peter Van Garderen (2016) has posited the notion of 'decentralized autonomous collections' (DACs) which he defines as 'a set of digital information objects stored for ongoing re-use with the means and incentives for independent parties to participate in the contribution, presentation, and curation of the information objects outside the control of an exclusive custodian'. Van Garderen's proposal sees DACs as an antidote to a number of the problems associated with traditional, centralised institutional repositories: shortage of resources, political interference and colonial attitudes. For Van Garderen, blockchain technology has the potential to displace traditional institutional archives as curators of digital content.

New proposals for digital curation and preservation using blockchain technology leave many questions unanswered. This is understandable with a technology that is so new. Research will be needed to:

- Determine how to evaluate the authenticity of records held in decentralised repositories
- Address who or what will ensure the long-term sustainability of decentralised, autonomous archives
- Understand how to incentivise nodes to sustainably participate in blockchain recordkeeping systems over time
- Determine how many nodes are needed to ensure authenticity of decentralised archives
- Figure out how to integrate centralised digital repositories with decentralised ones
- Address how cryptographically secured records will seamlessly transition to stronger cryptography over time to protect authenticity of records
- Determine the future for traditional memory institutions and archival professionals in the new world of decentralised, autonomous archives.

As with so many developments, in the next 30 to 40 years what transpires is likely to fall somewhere in between current practice and Van Garderen's radical prediction for the future of decentralised, autonomous digital content curation. That said, the overwhelming trend is towards a distributed, networked, autonomous and globalised future of records creation, use and storage. Archivists will need to come to grips with this new reality, regardless of the specific form of implementation it may take.

Archival education for a blockchain future

If blockchain technology is set to transform records creation and preservation, then records and archives professionals need to prepare themselves for a blockchain future. Recent reports have identified a global shortage of skilled technical workers to meet the demand for development of new blockchain solutions (Arnold, 2017). An equal number of skilled workers will be needed to advise on how to manage the creation and preservation of blockchain records in a way that guarantees authenticity and accessibility over the long-term. Will those skilled workers be records and archives professionals? Will they have any knowledge of archival theory and principles?

Perhaps not. For decades, archivists have been appraising, preserving and providing access to digital records using archival theories and methods developed for paper records with limited success. However, social and technical trends inform the production and use of records, which in the digital era means the use of information and computer technology and data science techniques (Marciano et al., 2018). These techniques have shown little or no connection to archival methods, often frustrating records and archives professionals' efforts to instantiate records controls that would ensure long-term authenticity and accessibility.

If computer scientists and engineers are laying claim to recordkeeping through the blockchain, then records and archives professionals need to claim it back for the future by asserting the value of archival knowledge when it comes to defining what produces trustworthy records over the long-term and, ultimately, through designing and implementing their vision for the future of this technology.

Does this mean that within the next 30 to 40 years archivists must become computer scientists or software engineers? Undoubtedly, records managers and archivists – or at least those that work on the management of current records or the preservation of digital ones – will become more adept at coding and more knowledgeable about computational methods. However, what is needed is a new trans-discipline which, at the same time as it draws records and archives professionals into the computational, draws computer scientists and software engineers into the archival, where an appreciation of the contextual nature of records may address a current tendency towards techno-solutionism.

This dialogue is starting to take shape in the form of 'computational archival science' (CAS). The definition of CAS is still unfolding, as is to be expected in an emerging knowledge area, and is currently described as:

> An interdisciplinary field concerned with the application of computational methods and resources to large-scale records/archives processing, analysis, storage, long-term preservation, and access, with the aim of improving efficiency, productivity and precision in support of appraisal, arrangement and description, preservation and access decisions.
>
> (Marciano et al., 2018)

The goal of CAS is to:

> … engage and undertake research with archival materials, as well as apply the collective knowledge of computer and archival science to understand the ways that new technologies change the generation, use, storage and preservation of records, and the implications of these changes for archival functions and the societal and organizational use and preservation of authentic digital records.
>
> (Marciano et al., 2018)

CAS is a blend of computational and archival thinking, which is what will be needed if records and archives professionals are to imbue emerging technical infrastructure with principles that reflect an understanding of the requirements for sustainable archival futures. It is a view of records and archives practice as defined by a shared common body of theory, not by the institutional location in which records and archives professionals practice their work nor the particular functions that they perform in doing so. Without this deep disciplinary integration, records and archives professionals may continue to work on the periphery or outside the boundaries of new technologies. They may rail against the disruptions novel technologies create, or the loss of memory, cultural heritage and evidence, but they may be ill-equipped to do much about these changes. They may have neither the technical skills nor be seen as legitimate actors able to intervene in the design of new technical infrastructures.

This version of the future is, perhaps, too dystopian. What may actually happen will probably be less extreme. But, this will only be the case if records and archives professionals engage more deeply with the computational. If they do not, the future as failure is more likely to be the case – failing themselves as professionals and failing posterity as the guardians of memory.

Conclusion

Archives and records professionals have made the transition into new recordkeeping futures before and they likely will make the transition again. They are not strangers to changes in modes of communication that impact upon how society makes and keeps records.

Given the rise of networks in human mental models, in social relations and in the material world, it is hard to imagine that the future of archives could be anything but networked, and thus also decentralised and autonomous. However, the specific form this may take is open to wide interpretation. Assuming the transformative influence of blockchain technology proves as great as some say it will be, then archives and records professionals are likely to see an ineluctable networked, decentralised and autonomous future manifest in the material form of blockchain recordkeeping systems. Archives and records professionals therefore must engage deeply with the computational to prepare for the future of archives.

The future is uncertain and cannot be known in advance with any degree of accuracy. What will transpire for the future of archives in the next 30 to 40 years may only become known just as humanity is on the verge of the next major shift in human thought and the changes to the social and material world that such a shift will bring about.

References

Arnold, M. (2017) Blockchain-related Job Adverts Surge, *Financial Times*, June 4, www.ft.com/content/e49e5310-4923-11e7-919a-1e14ce4af89b.

Briscoe, G. (2017) *Blockchain: distributed consensus protocols*, unpublished.

Castells, M. (1996) *The Rise of the Network Society, The Information Age: economy, society and culture*, Vol. I, Blackwell.

Clark, J. (2016) Foreword: The Long Road to Bitcoin. In Narayanan, A., Bonneau, J., Felton, E., Miller, A., and Goldfeder, S., *Bitcoin and Cryptocurrency Technologies*, Princeton University Press.

Lemieux, V. (2016) *Blockchain for Recordkeeping: help or hype?*, unpublished.

Lemieux, V. (2017) Evaluating the Use of Blockchain in Land Transactions: an archival science perspective, *European Journal of Property Law* (December 2017) 1–49.

Marciano, R., Lemieux, V., Hedges, M., Esteva, M., Underwood, W., Kurtz, M. and Conrad, M. (2018) Archival Records and Training in the Age of Big Data. In Percell, J., Sarin, L. C., Jaeger, P. and Bertot, J. C., *Re-Envisioning the MLS: Perspectives on the Future of Library and Information Science Education (Advances in Librarianship)*, Volume 44B, 179–99. NY: Emerald Publishing Ltd.

Nakamoto, S. (2008) *Bitcoin: A Peer-to-Peer Electronic Cash System*, unpublished.

Narayanan, A., Bonneau, J., Felton, E., Miller, A. and Goldfeder, S. (2016) *Bitcoin and Cryptocurrency Technologies*, Princeton University Press.

Pearce-Moses, R. (2017) *InterPARES Trust Terminology Database*, http://arstweb.clayton.edu/interlex/expandedSearch.php?term=authenticity.

Records in the Chain Project (2017) *Report on Use of Blockchain Technology in Medical Recordkeeping in Estonia*, unpublished.

Rosic, A. (2016) Ethereum vs Bitcoin: what's the main difference?, *Huffington Post*, last updated December 2017, www.huffingtonpost.com/ameer-rosic-/ethereum-vs-bitcoin-whats_b_13735404.html.

Seidel, M-D. (2017) Questioning Centralized Organizations in a Time of Distributed Trust, *Journal of Management Inquiry*, 1–5.

Snäll, M. (2017) Blockchain and Land Register – a new 'trust machine'?, *World Bank Land and Poverty Conference*, unpublished.

Szabo, N. (1997) The Idea of Smart Contracts, www.fon.hum.uva.nl/rob/Courses/InformationInSpeech/CDROM/Literature/LOTwinterschool2006/szabo.best.vwh.net/idea.html.

The TRUSTER Preservation Model (EU31), www.interparestrust.org/trust/about_research/studies.

Van Garderen, P. (2016) Decentralized Autonomous Collections, April 11, www.medium.com/on-archivy/decentralized-autonomous-collections-ff256267cbd6.

Walch, A. (2017) The Path of Blockchain Lexicon (and the Law), *Review of Banking & Financial Law*, **36**, 713–65.

4
_____

Can we keep everything? The future of appraisal in a world of digital profusion

Geoffrey Yeo

Introduction

This chapter asks whether we might begin to develop a vision of digital archives where nothing is ever destroyed. Today, proponents of 'big data' often argue that appraisal and selection are obsolescent. Can we – should we – try to keep everything, as many computing specialists now suggest? What place will selection and destruction practices have in a future digital world where storing everything may seem easier than incurring the costs and complexities of appraisal?

Selective retention

Decisions about destruction have been made since the earliest days of record-making. It has sometimes been thought that records in earlier times were intended to be permanent, and that keepers of records played no part in their destruction, until the practice of retaining everything had to be abandoned in the face of the growing physical bulk of records in the 20th century. Systematic destruction practices, however, have a much longer history. In the palaces and cities of the ancient world, accounting records were often routinely destroyed within a year of their creation (Eidem, 2011, 13; Palaima, 2003). In 1731, instructions were issued to the Royal Archives of Sardinia that 'useless papers' should be destroyed (Duchein, 1992, 17); three decades later, French archivist Pierre-Camille Le Moine similarly insisted on the destruction of seemingly trivial items (Delsalle, 1998, 154). In the UK, the Public Record Office Act of 1877 authorised the disposal of records thought insufficiently valuable (Cantwell, 1991, 277–80). The 20th-century appraisal methodologies articulated by Theodore Schellenberg (1956) formalised and encouraged these practices, but the origins of selectivity are much older.

Before digital technology became widely available, archival writers routinely put forward two arguments in favour of selective destruction: the need to save costly storage space and the difficulty of finding and using 'important' material if archives are congested with supposedly useless ephemera. These arguments appear in very similar form in the work of Charles Johnson in the early 20th century and in the writings of Gerald Ham in the century's final decade (Ham, 1993, 3; Johnson, 1919, 43–4). Although Hilary Jenkinson (1922) refused to allow the archivist any part in selection, many later writers saw a specific role for archivists in 'fashioning . . . a manageable historical record' (Ham, 1993, 3). The earliest records managers affirmed that 'the purpose of records management can be stated in simple terms: *fewer and better records*' (Leahy and Cameron, 1965, 17). Archivists, too, tended to believe that fewer records would equate to better records. To some, the volume of material presented problems that could be overcome only by 'rigorous selection' (Hall, 1908, 3); to others, the archivist's task was 'to preserve the clearest image possible of contemporary society . . . by choosing the best records' (Cook, 1991, 33).

In the early 21st century, these arguments were sometimes transferred to the new world of digital resources. Adrian Cunningham (2008, 535) argued against the preservation of 'mountains of . . . anarchic and unmanaged data' in favour of a 'mission to document the important things that happen in society and in public administration'. Ross Harvey (2008) also argued for a selective approach, on the grounds that 'selection and appraisal are key to ensuring that scientific data and records are usable and re-usable'. In Harvey's view, selectivity is a necessary response to the costs of storing and maintaining large quantities of digital data and offers benefits in terms of the quality of curation and the ability of archivists to demonstrate the trustworthiness of their holdings.

Nevertheless, there have been dissentient voices, especially among those who have examined archival appraisal and selection practices from the perspective of other disciplines. Among the most forceful critics was textual scholar Thomas Tanselle, who wrote that archivists:

> . . . often express the view that they have a duty to society, and to the future, to weed out insignificant material. The arrogance of this position is astounding. There is no way for anyone to know just which artifacts someone else, now or in the future, will find of significance; and there have . . . been innumerable instances of materials that were ignored at one time but highly prized at another.
>
> (Tanselle, 2002, 258)

Although Tanselle's strictures met with a hostile reception (Cox, 2004, 267–8), archivists are not unaware that both the aims and the methods of appraisal are highly controversial. Many archivists have remarked that appraisal and selection criteria are arbitrary and that appraisal exercises can be unpredictable, inconsistent and open to bias. Conducting appraisal by evaluating functions – proposed by several leading thinkers since the 1990s (Cook, 1992; Robyns, 2014) – seems no less subjective than directly evaluating records. For Mark Greene (2002), appraisal is an art, not a science. For others, beliefs that the purpose of appraisal is to identify records of 'the important things that happen in society' (Cunningham, 2008, 535) or 'the desired total image of society that should be left for posterity' (Cook, 1991, 33) are fraught with difficulty; they reveal archivists striving for the power to decide what is 'important' and manipulate future perceptions of the world.

A new perspective

For technologists, a critical issue is that digital storage has become ever cheaper. The cost of local disk storage in 2010 was a mere 1% of what it had been in 2000 and 0.001% of what it had been in 1990 (Komorowski, 2014). Today, cloud vendors offer digital storage at even lower cost or seemingly free of charge. As early as 2004, Google offered users of its Gmail service large quantities of 'free' storage and told them that 'you'll never need to delete another email' (Kirschenbaum, 2008, 98). In 2015, it announced that it would offer unlimited storage to most users of Google Apps (later re-named G-Suite). When the costs of large-scale storage are negligible – or at least so low that a cloud supplier can bundle them invisibly into the price charged for other services – we have effectively reached a point where, in most situations, upfront storage costs are no longer likely to influence decisions about retention.

One of the earliest fields of computer science research to build on notions of ever cheaper and more capacious digital storage was 'lifelogging': the use of technological tools to capture and retain supposedly complete records of individual lives. Originally based around wearable cameras and sensors, lifelogging initiatives expanded to imagine a future in which the totality of an individual's social media postings, text messages, emails and telephone conversations would be captured and stored alongside location data, images, ambient sounds and environmental measurements. Lifelogs might be further enhanced by integration with the so-called 'internet of things', offering the potential to record all the interactions we experience. Proponents argued that every record could be kept because storage costs would become minimal. The earliest lifelogging initiatives had little uptake, but computer science researchers have continued to work in this field and now often propose roles for lifelogging in personal wellbeing, reminiscence therapy or treatment of amnesia (Isaacs et al., 2013; Jones, 2014, 7–10).

A much greater amount of attention has been generated by 'big data': the exponential growth in the volumes of digital data that are produced and stored as computing devices proliferate across government, business and the wider community. The concept of big data enjoys a high profile, not least because of its perceived commercial potential for market research, decision-making and competitive advantage. It is characterised not only by data abundance, but also by the use of innovative computational techniques to analyse data on a scale previously impracticable, in the expectation of discovering patterns, trends or relationships that would otherwise remain unknown (Ernst and Young, 2014; Information Resources Management Association, 2016; Müller et al., 2016). Besides their use in the business world, these analytical techniques offer new opportunities for scholarly research (Thomas and Johnson, 2015).

In the 21st century, the use of data analytics has disrupted traditional thinking about the need for selectivity; instead of seeking to reduce data to manageable quantities, analysts now affirm that larger volumes of data produce better results and that the new techniques will be most effective if everything is kept and made available for analysis. As Kenneth Cukier and Viktor Mayer-Schoenberger explained, the world of big data requires us:

> . . . to collect and use a lot of data rather than settle for small amounts. . . . For most of history, people have worked with relatively small amounts of data because the tools for collecting, organizing, storing, and analyzing information were poor. People winnowed the information they relied on to the barest minimum so that they could examine it more easily . . . Today . . . we no longer need to rely on small samples.
> (Cukier and Mayer-Schoenberger, 2013)

In the past, we are told, human cognitive skills imposed limits on the quantities of data that could be assimilated, but large-scale retention becomes appropriate in a world where computer programs have much greater processing capabilities. Advocates of this approach insist that they 'never throw away data' and speak of organizations employing infinitely expandable digital 'data lakes' that will allow them to leverage all their data using search, data mining, text mining and other analytic tools derived from, or enhanced by, artificial intelligence (Davenport and Kim, 2013, 8; Losey, 2015).

Records professionals have often found these notions uncongenial. According to Terry Cook (1991, 33), 'even if archivists could keep everything, they should not do so'. Richard Cox contended that appraisal is still needed in digital environments and referred to ideas that selection is unnecessary as 'fantasies' (Cox, 2011; Cox and Larsen, 2008, 324). Reiterating the long-standing concerns about bulk and manageability, Lawrence Serewicz (2010) and Janet Knight and Kate Cumming (2012) also objected to proposals that everything should be kept, arguing that data volumes would grow beyond manageable levels. Kevin Dale (2015) suggested that records managers could assist 'big data' analysts by eliminating 'extraneous' data. Records professionals, as French historian Pierre Nora (1989, 14) observed, have 'learned that the essence of their trade is the art of controlled destruction', and they are understandably reluctant to abandon the art that has often seemed central to their professional identity.

A few voices within the records profession, however, have

suggested that traditional beliefs about the necessity of appraisal and destruction must now be revisited, and that ideas of keeping everything can no longer be dismissed as whimsical or unaffordable. Records manager Steve Bailey (2008, 100–2) remarked that emphasis on selective retention has become alien both to the computing industry and to popular culture, and that refusing to keep everything entails swimming against powerful currents in society. Anne Gilliland (2014, 54) followed Bailey's arguments and noted that keeping everything would offer better support for new modes of research. In a paper entitled 'Why we are moving to a world where we will keep everything forever', Barclay Blair (2015) affirmed that a fundamental shift towards total retention is now under way, regardless of whether records professionals approve or disapprove.

Archivists and records managers cannot ignore the social and technological trends that Bailey and Blair identified. Demands that everything be kept will not simply go away; indeed, they will probably become stronger. Over the next few years, we can expect to see growing debates about retention, into which records professionals will unavoidably be drawn. While we may still have concerns about the manageability of huge quantities of records, we must now consider the possibility that appraisal – as we knew it in the 20th century – is approaching its demise.

Feasibilities of change

Archives where nothing is destroyed may seem a challenging, perhaps even frightening, prospect. Conceptually, however, there are many reasons to commend them. Intact archival aggregations – aggregations that realise complete *fonds d'archives* – incur no loss of internal documentary context (Yeo, 2012, 79). If it is true that each record in an archival aggregation has networks of relationships with other records, and that 'the elimination of any record hurts the integrity of the archives' (Duranti, 2015, 28), keeping everything would prevent such damage. For those concerned about the fallibility of appraisal, it would remove the need for subjective decision-making. For those seeking archival inclusivity, it would end the privileging of certain voices – and the silencing of others – that occurs when archivists preserve records selectively.

There may also be more pragmatic reasons for retaining everything. As the pioneers of records management observed, 'selectivity is a long and arduous task' (Leahy and Cameron, 1965, 228), and it seems appropriate to consider whether preserving everything in digital form may now be less costly and less resource-intensive than undertaking detailed appraisal exercises. Of course, the major expense of digital preservation is not the cost of storage media but the cost of active ongoing preservation programmes; however, some preservation experts have argued that the cost barriers of such programmes are lower than was once thought (Gollins, 2009; Rosenthal, 2010). Although it was generally believed in the 1990s that digital preservation would be more expensive than preserving paper, at least one preservation initiative in the 2010s has found that unit costs of digital preservation are much lower than in paper settings (Mumma, Dingwall and Bigelow, 2011, 116).

It has also been found that eliminating digital traces is not easy. Identical or near-identical copies of digital records often proliferate across different storage media, and when one copy is destroyed it is rarely possible to be sure that no other copies exist. Forensic techniques can resurrect records that are thought to have been deleted. Sceptics may ask why we continue to incur the costs of appraisal in planning to destroy records, when technological milieux often make it impossible to ensure their complete elimination.

Nevertheless, a world where everything is kept would be a world with massive amounts of digital content. We are told that volumes of data grow at a rate of 40% per year (Information Resources Management Association, 2016, 1862) and that, by 2020, about 1.7 megabytes of data will be generated every second for every person on our planet (Kumar, 2017). These figures must be approximations, but the trends they indicate are unmistakable. Necessarily, archivists will question whether abandoning selection practices will be feasible when future quantities of material will exceed anything we have experienced in the past.

Even when unit costs of preservation are low, it is improbable that we will be able to preserve vast quantities of digital records unless new labour-saving techniques are introduced. Scaling up practices that depend heavily on manual effort is unlikely to be an option. However, digital preservation experts recognise a need to minimise dependence on human intervention and are working to automate curatorial tasks. Tools have been developed to automate tasks such as file format identification, migration, error correction and fixity checking, and these are increasingly being bundled into integrated packages to simplify preservation workflows. Because preservation specialists are aware that these tools and workflows may break down when faced with large or complex collections (King et al., 2012), they are actively exploring new automated approaches that will provide greater scalability, including the use of high-performance computing power (Arora, Esteva and Trelogan, 2014; Open Preservation Foundation, 2016). Researchers are also investigating the feasibility of automating the risk-detection, planning and monitoring processes that digital preservation requires (Becker, Faria and Duretec, 2014; Waddington et al., 2016).

Current preservation methods are best described as semi-automated, but in future we can expect to see more mature technologies that will enable preservation on a much bigger scale. Although high-performance computing and large-scale digital preservation have sometimes been viewed as environmentally unsustainable, computer scientists are actively developing new ways of reducing the environmental impact of technology (Rahman, 2016). Some digital preservation experts foresee a more distant time when digital objects will largely manage their own preservation and little human input will be needed except in policy-setting and oversight.

As advocates of selectivity have often noted, there can be no benefit in preserving large quantities of records that are undiscoverable or incomprehensible; further major challenges will arise in supplying the means to retrieve, interpret and contextualise the digital records of the future. Records professionals now have automated or semi-automated tools to extract *technical* metadata needed for digital preservation and access, but if large-scale retention is to be feasible they will also need to harness technology to generate *descriptive* metadata or find other ways of providing the traditional affordances of description. Manual descriptive work will be unable to keep pace with high volumes of digital records, and new computational approaches will be required.

It seems likely that, for much of this capability, records professionals will look to deploy the analytic tools for big data mentioned earlier in this chapter. Cloud storage providers have already started to offer their customers analytic tools enhanced by artificial intelligence (or 'cognitive computing') and machine-learning techniques, and many commentators believe that these tools are now becoming powerful enough to offer a basis for 'intelligent' digital archives and scalable records management (Shinkle, 2017). At a basic level, they can search text, identify subject terms, names and dates, map their frequency and uncover patterns and relationships among them; more advanced tools can attempt to detect references to activities or events and identify themes that are not explicit in textual content. Some aim to recognise the content of speech or audiovisual recordings, or objects in photographic images. Many offer the possibility of using the results of content analysis to classify digital records automatically into hierarchical categories like those used in traditional file-plans (Warland and Mokhtar, 2013), although it is increasingly acknow-ledged that imposing a single arrangement is inappropriate in digital domains, where records can be grouped and regrouped in different ways for different purposes (Yeo, 2017, 180–2). To help users explore large and complex aggregations, a variety of overviews can be generated through visualisation techniques (Whitelaw, 2015). Docu-mentation of records' interrelationships, and of their context or provenance, may also be semi-automatable using emerging com-putational methods (Lemieux, 2016; Spencer, 2017; Yeo, 2013).

Although many of these technologies are immature at present, they are developing rapidly; several recent studies have suggested that technology-assisted retrieval can be more accurate than manual approaches (Gricks and Ambrogi, 2015). However, extensive 'training' of the current generation of machine-learning systems is often required to achieve satisfactory results. The most fully developed systems are designed to support eDiscovery and investigation of their repurposing for archives is still in progress (The National Archives, 2016).

It is also evident that these technologies will have substantial cultural impacts, both for archivists and for users. For archivists, challenges will arise not only in acquiring the skills to apply computational approaches to archival processing, but also in integrating computational ideas with archival thinking (Marciano, 2016); many archivists will resist the notion of entrusting computers with tasks that have long been the domain of human judgement. For users of archives, computational approaches offer new opportunities for access and research, as Sonia Ranade contends in Chapter 6 of this book, but many of these opportunities will probably appeal more to scholars working in quantitative traditions than to those with qualitative or interpretative interests.

Of course, we cannot wholly foresee how these technologies will develop or how users will respond to them. Very probably, more transparent and user-friendly interfaces will be required before they can gain widespread trust and acceptance. Nevertheless, we can expect that, as the technologies mature, they will increasingly overcome the perceived difficulties of managing and using digital records on a large scale. While human input will still be needed, a greater level of reliance on computational tools will help us to control the digital deluge by facilitating work that would otherwise be impossibly laborious.

Retention transformed?

Let us return to the questions posed at the start of this chapter. In a world of digital profusion, where retention of records on a much larger scale is becoming possible and where many commentators see keeping everything as highly desirable, what will be the future for appraisal and selection? In the archives of tomorrow, will we indeed aspire to preserve everything?

Prima facie, total retention still seems unlikely. Almost inevitably, just as in the pre-digital world, some records will continue to be lost through failure, or disinclination, to maintain them. As Catherine Marshall (2008) observed, it will remain natural 'to lose a certain amount of one's digital stuff to the forces of benign neglect'.

At least in the short-to-medium term, losses will also continue to result from considered decision-making. It is not yet easy to imagine a time when we will completely escape from the need to restrict preservation because of constraints on computing power, storage capacity or management resources. Although non-selective retention will become increasingly common, cost factors will almost certainly mean that some selection decisions remain unavoidable. Consider a few examples from the current world of truly 'big' data:

- In 2012, CERN (the European Organization for Nuclear Research) processed 300,000 megabytes of data from its Large Hadron Collider every second; quantities in later years have been even greater. CERN applies selection algorithms to the data at the time of processing; in 2012, only 0.1% were kept. Nevertheless, the preserved data amounted to 15 million gigabytes in a year (Borek et al., 2014, 34). Given that keeping the other 99.9% every year would notionally have required CERN to expand its storage capacity – in more than ten data centres across Europe – to the equivalent of over 10,000 data centres, it must be doubted whether even the keenest preservation advocates could have persuaded CERN to embrace total retention.

- It has been estimated that 86% of email messages are unsolicited 'spam' and that about 400 billion spam messages are sent every day (Robertson, 2016). Even if these messages might be usable in a research project sometime in the future, it would seem difficult to construct a satisfactory business case for preserving them.
- Several years after agreeing to 'preserve every tweet ever posted', the US Library of Congress found that it remained unable to provide public access to its 'Twitter archive'. The numbers of tweets hugely exceeded the library's expectations and the engineering challenges of managing them and making them accessible were beyond its resources (McGill, 2016).

In the immediate future, we will not keep everything that is created digitally. We will not consider it worthwhile to configure every database so that every change is captured for posterity, and preservation on the very largest scale will demand resources that most archival institutions are unlikely to possess. The volume of digital material will still necessitate some kind of appraisal activity to determine what is to be preserved, even if (as at CERN) the appraisal is performed by algorithms rather than human agents. Of course, some archivists might argue that tweets, spam emails and CERN's experimental data are not *records*. They are certainly not what I have elsewhere called *prototypical* records: the sort of records that most closely match our mental image of archival holdings (Yeo, 2008). But questions of what constitutes a record are notoriously slippery; deciding whether particular classes of digital objects are or are not records is itself a kind of appraisal decision.

Nevertheless, archivists should expect to keep much larger quantities of records in future than they have been able to keep in the past. Over time, as technological tools to support preservation, description and access become more sophisticated and widely available, the kinds of difficulties the Library of Congress faced with the 'Twitter archive' will almost certainly diminish and eventually disappear. Human intervention will not cease to be necessary, but it will be focused on those aspects of curation that depend on personalised advocacy or the highest levels of what Jenny Bunn (in Chapter 5 of this book) calls sense-making. When this happens, large-scale retention will no longer seem so daunting, and – especially where prototypical organizational or personal records are concerned – keeping all, rather than keeping only some, will become a normal if not universal professional practice.

Appraisal exercises will not vanish, but their aims and scope will be different. In many settings, appraisal will be more concerned with determining what records should be created (what kind of events should be documented; what kind of questions or commitments should be put in writing) than with determining what records should be selected for preservation. Records professionals will have a continuing role in verifying that records are created and secured appropriately. They will still need to ensure that accountability and transparency are not impeded by individuals or organizations evading the creation of records or concealing or destroying records to avoid liability or disclosure of embarrassing information. In most organizations, there will also be a continuing place for work we might call appraisal in determining what records need to be moved from operational systems to inactive storage or in identifying records that require additional security. Some of these tasks may be automatable, but they remain appraisal – or appraisal-like – tasks that records professionals will wish to oversee.

In many archival institutions, we can expect that appraisal will be focused on identifying recordkeeping systems – or collections, if we prefer more traditional terminology – for acquisition; we can also expect that far more acquisitions will be accepted than in the past. Some collecting institutions may find that they no longer need to reject any digital collections they are offered and that they can indeed 'keep everything'. Even where acceptance remains selective, we will see appraisal and selection *of* collections rather than *within* collections. There will be no place for weeding collections or for most other forms of item-level or file-level appraisal. Sampling, often advocated in the past as an approach to selective preservation (Cook, 1991; Neumayer and Rauber, 2007), will also become a rarity; it will probably still be needed where records or data are created on an industrial scale, as at CERN, but sampling of records of administrative processes (known to archivists as 'case records' or 'particular instance records') will be outmoded.

An important exception to this picture of near-total retention relates to issues of privacy and confidentiality. Privacy legislation – such as European data protection laws – may mandate the selective destruction of records relating to named individuals. The movement towards keeping everything must be tempered by legislation of this kind, just as it must be tempered by the growing acknowledgement that individuals in modern societies may, more problematically, have a 'right to be forgotten'. As Gilliland (2014, 54) observed, there will still be 'supportable rationales' for selective destruction when sensitive human rights issues are at stake. When legal or moral requirements for destruction are thought to be absent, procedures may still be needed to identify records that are deemed sensitive, but such records can be redacted or kept inaccessible for an appropriate time period rather than being destroyed. Institutions faced with the task of discovering sensitive content within large-scale digital holdings are increasingly turning to computational techniques to assist review (Baron and Borden, 2016; Moss, 2015, 9–11).

Finally, records professionals who continue to see a role for appraisal in identifying and selecting 'the few gems that have value' (Cook, 1991, 45) among mountainous quantities of records will still be able to draw attention to items of perceived importance within large-scale aggregations, if they wish. It is not difficult to imagine future interfaces that could offer users the choice of exploring the whole of a vast accumulation of digital records or of viewing only an archivist's chosen selection. Indeed, an archival institution could offer more than one selection; users interested in a particular theme or topic could be invited to view selection A, while users with other interests could examine selections B, C or D. Users could also be empowered to make their own selections and publish them alongside the archivist's selections for the benefit of other users in the future. For users reluctant to rely on computational methods of retrieval, online systems offering preconfigured selections would provide alternative means of finding material that might otherwise seem to be hidden from view in large and congested archives. Although all such selections would be subjective, records professionals would be able to apply their appraisal skills in constructing them. However, this approach would differ from traditional appraisal in one crucial respect: it would not lead to the destruction of the unselected records. Archives in their entirety would remain available for inspection and analysis, and users would be free to disregard the choices that records professionals had made.

Conclusion

Attempting to predict the future is always risky. Although it seems certain that the great majority of records will be created in digital form, we do not know how far paper or other pre-digital media will remain in use in coming decades. We cannot foretell what other new forms of technology will evolve or how they may affect the making and keeping of records. But it has become evident that archivists in the future will encounter records in unprecedented quantities; many more records will be made, and many more will be kept, than in the analogue world of the past.

Even if we cannot or will not preserve every single record of human endeavour, a shift to keeping digital records on a much larger scale will require a major transformation of professional thinking and practice. It will not only oblige us to let go of long-favoured ideas about the need for highly selective retention but will also affect how we undertake other archival functions such as description and access. We should consider large-scale retention not as a pipedream or a capitulation to the values of technology enthusiasts, but as an opportunity to expand the scope and utility of the archives of the future. Nevertheless, we must recognise that it will be a disruptive force impelling us to develop more robust practices for the coming world of digital profusion. At present, the tools we will need are still emerging and much remains unclear about the ways in which we will use these tools and acquire confidence in them. As yet, we also have little understanding of the cultural and emotional responses that use of the new tools will evoke. We should not underestimate the intellectual and practical challenges these changes will bring, but investigating and embracing them must be the way ahead for the records profession as it faces the digital deluge of the 21st century.

References

Arora, R., Esteva, M. and Trelogan, J. (2014) Leveraging High Performance Computing for Managing Large and Evolving Data Collections, *International Journal of Digital Curation*, **9** (2), 17–27.

Bailey, S. (2008) *Managing the Crowd: rethinking records management for the Web 2.0 world*, Facet Publishing.

Baron, J.R. and Borden, B.B. (2016) *Opening Up Dark Digital Archives through the Use of Analytics to Identify Sensitive Content*, http://dcicblog.umd.edu/cas/wp-content/uploads/sites/13/2016/05/3.pdf.

Becker, C., Faria, L. and Duretec, K. (2014) Scalable Decision Support for Digital Preservation, *OCLC Systems & Services*, **30** (4), 249–84.

Blair, B.T. (2015) *Why We Are Moving to a World Where We Will Keep Everything Forever*, www.linkedin.com/pulse/why-we-moving-world-where-keep-everything-forever-barclay-t-blair.

Borek, A., Parlikad, A.K., Webb, J. and Woodall, P. (2014) *Total Information Risk Management*, Morgan Kaufmann.

Cantwell, J.D. (1991) *The Public Record Office 1838–1958*, HMSO.

Cook, T. (1991) 'Many Are Called, but Few Are Chosen'? Appraisal guidelines for sampling and selecting case files, *Archivaria*, **32**, 25–50.

Cook, T. (1992) Mind over Matter: towards a new theory of archival appraisal. In Craig, B.L. (ed.), *The Archival Imagination: essays in honour of Hugh A. Taylor*, Association of Canadian Archivists.

Cox, R.J. (2004) *No Innocent Deposits: forming archives by rethinking appraisal*, Scarecrow Press.

Cox, R.J. (2011) Appraisal and the Future of Archives in the Digital Era. In Hill, J. (ed.), *The Future of Archives and Recordkeeping*, Facet Publishing.

Cox, R.J. and Larsen, R.L. (2008) iSchools and Archival Studies, *Archival Science*, **8** (4), 307–26.

Cukier, K.N. and Mayer-Schoenberger, V. (2013) The Rise of Big Data: how it's changing the way we think about the world, *Foreign Affairs*, **92** (3), www.foreignaffairs.com/articles/2013-04-03/rise-big-data.

Cunningham, A. (2008) Digital Curation/Digital Archiving: a view from the National Archives of Australia, *American Archivist*, **71** (2), 530–43.

Dale, K.L. (2015) RIM's Role in Harnessing the Power of Big Data,

Information Management, **49** (4), 29–32.

Davenport, T.H. and Kim, J. (2013) *Keeping Up with the Quants: your guide to understanding and using analytics,* Harvard Business School.

Delsalle, P. (1998) *Une Histoire de L'archivistique,* Presses de l'Université du Québec.

Duchein, M. (1992) The History of European Archives and the Development of the European Archival Profession, *American Archivist,* **55** (1), 14–25.

Duranti, L. (2015) Archival Bond. In Duranti, L. and Franks, P.C. (eds), *Encyclopedia of Archival Science,* Rowman & Littlefield.

Eidem, J. (2011) *The Royal Archives from Tell Leilan,* Nederlands Instituut voor het Nabije Oosten.

Ernst and Young Global Ltd (2014) *Big Data: changing the way businesses compete and operate,* www.ey.com/Publication/vwLUAssets/EY_-_Big_data:_changing_the_way_businesses_operate/%24FILE/EY-Insights-on-GRC-Big-data.pdf.

Gilliland, A.J. (2014) Archival Appraisal: practising on shifting sands. In Brown, C. (ed.), *Archives and Recordkeeping: theory into practice,* Facet Publishing.

Gollins, T. (2009) *Parsimonious Preservation: preventing pointless processes,* www.nationalarchives.gov.uk/documents/information-management/parsimonious-preservation.pdf.

Greene, M.A. (2002) *Not Magic, not Science, but Art: comment on 'Archival Appraisal Alchemy' (response to Richard Cox),* http://web.archive.org/web/20041217002026/http://www.hfmgv.org/research/publications/symposium2002/papers/greene.asp.

Gricks, T.C. and Ambrogi, R.J. (2015) *A Brief History of Technology Assisted Review,* www.lawtechnologytoday.org/2015/11/history-technology-assisted-review.

Hall, H. (1908) *Studies in English Official Historical Documents,* Cambridge University Press.

Ham, F.G. (1993) *Selecting and Appraising Archives and Manuscripts,* Society of American Archivists.

Harvey, R. (2008) *Appraisal and Selection,* www.dcc.ac.uk/resources/briefing-papers/introduction-curation/appraisal-and-selection.

Information Resources Management Association (2016) *Big Data: concepts, methodologies, tools, and applications,* IGI Global.

Isaacs, E., Konrad, A., Walendowski, A., Lennig, T., Hollis, V. and Whittaker, S. (2013) Echoes from the Past: how technology mediated reflection improves well-being. In *CHI '13: Proceedings of the SIGCHI Conference on Human Factors in Computing Systems*, ACM Press.

Jenkinson, H. (1922) *A Manual of Archive Administration*, Clarendon Press.

Johnson, C. (1919) *The Care of Documents and Management of Archives*, SPCK.

Jones, W. (2014) *Transforming Technologies to Manage Our Information: the future of personal information management*, Vol.2, Morgan and Claypool.

King, R., Schmidt, R., Becker, C. and Schlarb, S. (2012) SCAPE: big data meets digital preservation, *ERCIM News*, **89**, 30–1.

Kirschenbaum, M.G. (2008) *Mechanisms: new media and the forensic imagination*, MIT Press.

Knight, J. and Cumming, K. (2012) Digital Data Hoarding and the Implications for RIM Professionals, *IQ: the RIM quarterly*, **28** (3), 32–5.

Komorowski, M. (2014) *A History of Storage Cost*, www.mkomo.com/cost-per-gigabyte.

Kumar, V. (2017) *Big Data Facts*, www.analyticsweek.com/content/big-data-facts.

Leahy, E.J. and Cameron, C.A. (1965) *Modern Records Management*, McGraw-Hill.

Lemieux, V.L. (2016) Provenance: past, present and future in interdisciplinary and multidisciplinary perspective. In Lemieux, V.L. (ed.), *Building Trust in Information: perspectives on the frontiers of provenance*, Springer.

Losey, R. (2015) *Information Governance v Search: the battle lines are redrawn*, www.e-discoveryteam.com/2015/02/08/information-governance-v-search-the-battle-lines-are-redrawn.

Marciano, R. (2016) *Building a 'Computational Archival Science' Community*, www.saaers.wordpress.com/2016/07/27/building-a-computational-archival-science-community.

Marshall, C.C. (2008) Rethinking Personal Digital Archiving Part 2: implications for services, applications, and institutions, *D-Lib Magazine*, **14** (3–4), www.dlib.org/dlib/march08/marshall/03marshall-pt2.html.

McGill, A. (2016) *Can Twitter Fit Inside the Library of Congress?*, www.theatlantic.com/technology/archive/2016/08/can-twitter-fit-inside-the-library-of-congress/494339.

Moss, M. (2015) What is the Same and What is Different. In Moss, M. and Endicott-Popovsky, B. (eds) *Is Digital Different?*, Facet Publishing.

Müller, O., Junglas, I., vom Brocke, J. and Debortoli, S. (2016) Utilizing Big Data Analytics for Information Systems Research: challenges, promises and guidelines, *European Journal of Information Systems*, **25**, 289–302.

Mumma, C.C., Dingwall, G. and Bigelow, S. (2011) A First Look at the Acquisition and Appraisal of the 2010 Olympic and Paralympic Winter Games Fonds: or, SELECT * FROM VANOC_Records AS archives WHERE value="true";, *Archivaria*, **72**, 93–122.

Neumayer, R. and Rauber, A. (2007) *Why Appraisal is not 'Utterly' Useless and Why It's Not the Way to Go Either*, www.ifs.tuwien.ac.at/~neumayer/pubs/NEU07_appraisal.pdf.

Nora, P. (1989) Between Memory and History: les lieux de mémoire, *Representations*, **26**, 7–24.

Open Preservation Foundation (2016) *Introducing E-ARK Specifications and the E-ARK Web Platform*, www.openpreservation.org/event/introducing-e-ark-specifications-and-the-e-ark-web-platform.

Palaima, T. (2003) Archives and Scribes and Information Hierarchy in Mycenaean Greek Linear B Records. In Brosius, M. (ed.), *Ancient Archives and Archival Traditions*, Oxford University Press.

Rahman, N. (2016) Toward Achieving Environmental Sustainability in the Computer Industry, *International Journal of Green Computing*, **7** (1), 37–54.

Robertson, J. (2016) *E-Mail Spam Goes Artisanal*, www.bloomberg.com/news/articles/2016-01-19/e-mail-spam-goes-artisanal.

Robyns, M.C. (2014) *Using Functional Analysis in Archival Appraisal*, Rowman & Littlefield.

Rosenthal, D.S.H. (2010) Format Obsolescence: assessing the threat and the defences, *Library Hi Tech*, **28** (2), 195–210.

Schellenberg, T.R. (1956) *Modern Archives: principles and techniques*, F.W. Cheshire.

Serewicz, L.W. (2010) Do We Need Bigger Buckets or Better Search Engines? The challenge of unlimited storage and semantic web search for records management, *Records Management Journal*, **20** (2), 172–81.

Shinkle, T. (2017) Automated Electronic Records Management: are we there yet?, *IRMS Bulletin*, **197**, 14–20.

Spencer, R. (2017) Binary Trees? Automatically identifying the links between born-digital records, *Archives and Manuscripts*, **45** (2), 77–99.

Tanselle, G.T. (2002) The Librarians' Double-Cross, *Raritan*, **21** (4), 245–63.

The National Archives [of the UK] (2016) *The Application of Technology-Assisted Review to Born-Digital Records Transfer, Inquiries and Beyond*, www.nationalarchives.gov.uk/documents/technology-assisted-review-to-born-digital-records-transfer.pdf.

Thomas, D. and Johnson, V. (2015) From the Library of Alexandria to the Google Campus: has the digital changed the way we do research? In Moss, M. and Endicott-Popovsky, B. (eds) *Is Digital Different?*, Facet Publishing.

Waddington, S., Hedges, M., Riga, M., Mitzias, P., Kontopoulos, E., Kompatsiaris, I., Vion-Dury, J., Lagos, N., Darányi, S., Corubolo, F., Muller, C. and McNeill, J. (2016) *PERICLES: digital preservation through management of change in evolving ecosystems*, www.pmitzias.com/publications/PERICLES_Digital_Preservation_ through_Management_of_Change_in_Evolving_Ecosystems.pdf.

Warland, A. and Mokhtar, U.A. (2013) Can Technology Classify Records Better than a Human?, *IRMS Bulletin*, **171**, 16–19.

Whitelaw, M. (2015) Representing Digital Collections. In Carlin, D. and Vaughan, L. (eds) *Performing Digital: multiple perspectives on a living archive*, Ashgate.

Yeo, G. (2008) Concepts of Record (2): prototypes and boundary objects, *American Archivist*, **71** (1), 118–43.

Yeo, G. (2012) The Conceptual Fonds and the Physical Collection, *Archivaria*, **73**, 43–80.

Yeo, G. (2013) Trust and Context in Cyberspace, *Archives and Records*, **34** (2), 214–34.

Yeo, G. (2017) Continuing Debates about Description. In MacNeil, H. and Eastwood, T. (eds) *Currents of Archival Thinking*, 2nd edn, Libraries Unlimited.

5

Frames and the future of archival processing

Jenny Bunn

Introduction

In 1989, David Bearman published an essay entitled 'Archival Methods' in which he set out a comparison between the magnitude of the tasks archivists had set themselves and the magnitude of their capabilities, revealing 'substantial discrepancies' (Bearman, 1989). Revisiting this work in 1995, he noted that: 'No one has directly disputed the claim that our methods are out of sync with the problems by more than an order of magnitude' (Bearman, 1995, 381–2). Indeed, in 2005, a very similar claim was made by Mark Greene and Dennis Meissner who stated that: 'Processing backlogs continue to be a problem for archivists, and yet the problem is exacerbated by many of the traditional approaches to processing collections that archivists continue to practice' (Greene and Meissner, 2005, 208). They too, as Bearman had done, called for archivists to think again about their methods and made suggestions for new approaches.

The suggestion, in 1989, 1995 and 2005, was that traditional archival methods were inadequate; they could not hope to succeed given the scale of the task at hand and needed to change. It is now over 12 years later and yet it would be very easy for this chapter to become just another instance of the same: a stark reminder of the ever-increasing magnitude and difficulty of the archival task, a call to rethink and some suggestions for how to proceed. In striving to avoid this easy path, this chapter will instead seek to cover the ground from a slightly different angle by exploring some of the solutions that have been proposed by others and using them as a starting point for a discussion about the future of archival processing.

In the above, the terms archival methods and archival processing have been used interchangeably and there is a broad sense in which both can be taken to mean all the things that archivists do: their activities, their processes, their methods. Archivists undertake many different processes, however, and the Society of American Archivists' glossary narrows its definition of processing down to the 'arrangement, description, and housing of archival materials for storage and use by patrons', although it also notes that 'Some archives include accessioning as part of processing' (Society of American Archivists, n.d.). The solutions which are being used as our starting point would seem to imply a mix of both senses, broad and narrow.

For example, one solution implying the more general sense is that offered by Greene and Meissner. They suggest that it would be 'a sign of professional maturity' if archivists were 'to own up to the limitations we work under and accept that the golden minimum recommended here . . . is all we can realistically accomplish' (Greene and Meissner, 2005, 255). Sensible advice to be sure, which could apply equally well to all forms of work, but in these times of increasingly constrained resources, this has become less a solution than a reality for the many archivists who are only too aware of the need to 'make each new situation argue for any additional investment of time and effort' (Greene and Meissner, 2005, 248).

On the other hand, a solution which seems to suggest processing in a narrower sense, of carrying out description, is that suggested by David Bearman in 1995 that archivists should 'Let Users Describe Records' (1995, 402). Much has been written about such user-generated description in recent years, particularly as new technologies have allowed it to morph into the field of crowdsourcing, and this is another solution that has become a reality, at least to some extent.

In this chapter we will be starting from the point of proposed solutions to the challenges faced by archival processing (in both the broad and narrow sense), but this is not where we will be ending up. We will not be providing detailed suggestions for how we can alter the processes of archivists to cope with the vast scale of the task they face. Instead, we will be considering solutions already proposed in order to unpick the framings and meanings of archival processing implied by those solutions: the ways in which we characterise what archival processing involves. We shall do so in the hope that this will lead to a better understanding of the fact that we can frame archival processing and the problems it faces in many different ways. Perhaps understanding this will provide another type of solution, one which allows us to imagine different futures and framings and to avoid treading the same paths again and again?

Un-framing archival processing: moving information across systems

The solution we will use as our starting point is the suggestion made by David Bearman that 'archivists will need to identify that information which can be obtained from outside, and import it into their systems automatically' (1989). Archivists have always obtained and imported information from outside into their systems, but that process was not, until very recently, an automatic one. Previously, if an archivist wished to import, say, the information written on a file cover into one of their systems, such as the catalogue which detailed their holding of said file, it was generally a process of manual re-typing. Now the information on the file cover comes instead in the digital form of a standard binary code, such that a quick press of a button and a machine will have imported into archival systems a list of possibly hundreds of thousands of files, along with lots of other information about them, such as size and dates created and modified. Tools, such as DROID, have already been developed and are increasingly being adopted by archivists to carry out this task, with the added bonus of the automatic generation and importing of new information, such as a checksum to fix each file's integrity.

What sort of framing and meaning of archival processing is implied by this solution? Firstly, as the above discussion makes clear, one of the framings it implies is a distinction between manual and automatic processing and an assumption that the automation of processes will make those processes more efficient. This assumption may well be correct, but that is an argument that can be had in relation to all types of processes, not just archival ones. Secondly then, and in a way that speaks more to the definition of the sort of processes that are involved in archival processing, it frames the activity it describes as importing information from external systems into internal systems.

Moving information across different systems is not always as seamless and as easy a process as we think it should be. As Duff and Harris remind us: 'Early twenty-first-century technological realities make it impossible to build a complex collective project without standards. For example, every e-mail message relies on over 200 internet standards for its successful transmission' (Duff and Harris, 2002, 283). This complexity, the legs paddling furiously beneath the swan gliding across the water, can most easily be seen through a focus on interoperability. A detailed look at this issue, from a recordkeeping metadata perspective, has been undertaken by Joanne Evans (2007). One of the lenses that Evans employs in her consideration of interoperability is provided by the Layers of Interoperability Model. This model sees an abstract layer supported by a representation layer supported by a transport and exchange layer.

As Evans writes, 'underpinning this abstract layer is a conceptual data model' (2007, 50). The need for such underpinnings highlights the way in which what is ultimately being transported and exchanged is not just data, or in this case metadata, but the meaning and understanding of that (meta)data. Such meaning and understanding depends on also understanding 'the perspective or context of metadata' and it is this that the conceptual data model sets out (Evans, 2007, 50).

With the development of the new Records in Contexts standard, archivists are attempting to create such a conceptual data model; a setting out of the important entities in the archival world view (e.g. records, agents, functions, dates) and the ways in which they are or can be related. The intention is that this model will also be encoded in the form of an ontology, such that it will be understandable to computers as well as human beings (International Council on Archives Experts Group on Archival Description, 2016). This last point raises again the distinction between manual and automatic processing, albeit in the form of human versus computer processing.

The framing of moving information across different systems also raises the question of the framing of those systems. Do we see just them in terms of different software packages, or do we take a wider view? What if you see them less as pieces of software and more as 'interdependent components organized to achieve an end ... organized collections of hardware, software, supplies, people, policies and procedures, and all the maintenance and training that are required to keep these components working together' (Bearman, 1993, 17). In this light, we might conceive of a system as an entire society, era or epoch, and the information we are moving across those systems as an understanding of those past societies, eras and epochs, such that they inter-operate with our own. Our view of archival processing would again be a wider one, seeing it more in terms of everything that archivists do, their very purpose and point, not just (meta)data automatically imported or not.

Perhaps then, another aspect of archival processing that this un-framing suggests is that the seemingly easy slippage between its broad and narrow senses is not just a question of whether accessioning is or is not a part of archival processing, but rather an indication of a deep connection between that processing and the purpose it serves?

Un-framing archival processing: documenting records-creating

So far, I have suggested that the frame for archival processing implied in the suggested solution that 'archivists will need to identify that information which can be obtained from outside, and import it into their systems automatically' is that archival processing can be conceived of in terms of moving information across different systems (Bearman, 1989).

I have surfaced the way in which such a conception can work in terms of both wider and narrower senses of archival processing, as everything that archivists do or just the management of metadata, and I have highlighted the distinction between manual and automatic processing that is implicit within this frame. I shall now turn to another suggested solution, that made by David Bearman, that 'archives should not describe records, but, rather, document records-creating activity' (1995, 401).

Within this solution there is clearly another distinction being used as a frame, this time it is not that between manual and automatic processing but rather that between description and documentation. This distinction is also discussed by Bearman in the article, 'Documenting Documentation' (1992). Here he explains it in terms of focus, stating that whereas 'Description is focused on records . . . Documentation is focused on activity in the records-generating institution' (Bearman, 1992, 34). Later in the article he expands on his definition of this last activity as 'the activity that generated the records, the organizations and individuals who used the records, and the purposes to which the records were put' (1992, 45).

Whereas Bearman's phrasing seems to suggest that the focus should not be on the records at all, current recordkeeping standards suggest that the focus should be on both the records and on certain aspects of records-creating activity. For example, ISO 23081-2:2009 suggests that entities of particular importance are:

> the records themselves, whether an individual document or aggregations of records . . .
> the people or organizing structures in the business environment . . .
> the business transacted . . .
> the rules governing the transaction and documentation of business . . .
> (ISO 23081-2:2009, 7)

The recent consultation draft of the Records in Contexts conceptual model brings into focus even more entities, providing a list of: record, record component, record set, agent, occupation, position, function, function (abstract), activity, mandate, documentary form, date, place and concept/thing (International Council on Archives Experts Group on Archival Description, 2016).

Viewed in these terms, what becomes most clear is the scale and magnitude of the archival processing task. For in these terms, archival processing becomes framed as the process of keeping track of and recording details about all these kinds of entities and how they are related. Worse still, if archival processing in these terms is set against the frame of needing to do this in a way that makes the resulting information available for automatic processing by computers (across different systems), that scale and magnitude leaps to a whole new level. In the past, human processing by archivists led to the creation of a reasonably efficient summary of this sort of information in the form of narrative description or text which could easily be processed by other humans (assuming that they spoke the same language). Even so Greene and Meissner were concerned that:

An unfortunate tendency on the part of processing archivists is to use the preparation of these text notes as an excuse to demonstrate their own knowledge (of both collection and historical context) and writing ability. Perhaps this is an attempt to demonstrate professionalism but, if so, it is a misguided one that further reduces processing productivity. The goal should always be to convey such narrative content and contextual information as briefly as possible and with as little recourse to outside sources as possible.   (Greene and Meissner, 2005, 247)

And yet, despite Greene and Meissner's misgivings, I would suggest that this process of summary (dealing with all the different entities as part of one narrative) text production (and occasionally translation into other human languages) is still less labour intensive than what seems to now be required: creating separate descriptions for all the different sorts of entities involved, linking them together, encoding them all in machine readable form, developing the computer systems to store, process and display the resulting data and agreeing on the standards, ontologies and conceptual data models by which it will all be interoperable and portable as one short-lived digital technology is replaced by another short-lived digital technology.

Un-framing archival processing: information processing

In the previous section, I suggested that the frame for archival processing implied in the suggested solution that 'archives should not describe records, but, rather, document records-creating activity' (Bearman, 1995, 401) is that archival processing can be conceived of in terms of keeping track of and recording information on a large number of different sorts of entities and the relationships between them. I have surfaced how this task is complicated when it can no longer be completed solely by summary text production but needs instead to be undertaken in a way that also makes the resulting information available for automatic processing by computers. It is not my intention, however, to give the impression that computers are therefore the problem. Rather, the previous discussion is intended to lead into one more un-framing of archival processing, this time one which sees it in terms of information processing.

Information processing is defined by the Oxford English Dictionary

(2018) as 'the processing (by a machine or by an organism) so as to yield new or more useful information'. As the definition makes clear, it is something that is done by both living and non-living things, by both humans and computers. However, the ways in which they undertake that processing is different. To indicate this difference, I will refer to information processing in respect of computer information processing, but sense-making in respect of human information processing. This is not to suggest that sense-making and information processing are necessarily the same thing, but that I believe human information processing to be qualitatively different to that undertaken by computers.

In Bearman's initial framing of the problem which started this article, certain 'costly and inefficient steps' in archival methods were identified by name, these being those 'of analysing the records themselves in order to find clues to context, and then entering this data into our own descriptive systems by keyboard' (Bearman, 1989). Any archivist who has processed material, looking through the detritus of other people's lives in order to find and read those clues and make sense of what they are seeing for themselves and others, will tell you that it is time-consuming and difficult. But does that necessarily make it costly and inefficient? Depending on how much the archivist is being paid it could be costly, but is it inefficient? Is this specific kind of information processing, of sense-making, something that a computer, an automatic rather than a manual processor, could do better, faster or more efficiently?

Sense-making

In highlighting this process, I do not assert that it is one solely undertaken by archivists and records managers. Historians and researchers, groups from which archivists and records managers sometimes individually, and increasingly as a professional collective, feel the need to make a definitional difference, also undertake such readings of archival material (albeit mostly readings of material that has already been processed by archivists to some degree). For example, Liz Stanley, coming from a research perspective, talks in terms of archigraphics, and the development of 'an archival sensibility', as well as processes of questioning, mapping, documentary analysis and interpretation (Stanley, 2017). Then again, Jennifer Meehan, coming from the archival perspective, talks in terms of 'an analytical process' involving 'acts of interpretation and representation' with reference to the idea of inference (Meehan, 2009, 72–3). This is the process to which I am referring and the terms in which I see archival processing as a form of sense-making.

Returning then to the question of whether this process can be carried out more efficiently by a computer than a human being, one variable that is hugely important is the nature of the material on which the process is being carried out. For, if it is not digital in nature, the computer will not be able to process it at all and the human being is the only option. Increasingly though, the nature of the material we are working with is changing as it is born-digital. With this change, the sort of clues that archivists had become expert at reading, such as changes in format or patterns of organization, may no longer exist in the same way and may no longer be discernible without help. Is one reason why we tend not to surface this process of sense-making within archival processing very often because we know we have lost it? If so, do we want to prevaricate until this loss leaves us in danger of becoming useless or do we want to relearn it? How can we combine the computer's information processing, admittedly faster and more accurate as it is over large quantities of digital material, with our own sense-making?

This question is very much an open one, but there have been projects that have considered it. For example, innovative research carried out by Kathryn Chandler as part of a Masters of Archival Studies at the University of British Columbia, has explored the potential of using new tools for exactly the sort of archival sense-making that has been discussed above (Chandler, 2016). These tools allowed for the extraction of certain pieces of data from a data set and then the running of this data through several community detection algorithms to produce visualisations of putative communities, or social networks, within a single department at the University. These visualisations were not the end-point of the research, but were rather the starting point for a process of sense matching in which the senses of the (net)working within the department produced by the algorithms in the form of visualisations were matched (or not) against the senses of the same as they were experienced by those working within that department (Chandler, 2017, 271).

Members of staff within the department were asked which of the visualisations 'best reflected their pattern of record modification' and the manager was asked which 'best represented the department' (Chandler, 2017, 271). In this way, Chandler was able to explore a number of things including: (a) in the new digital environment, the effectiveness of clues, such as the names of agents and the dates of actions, traditionally relied on by archivists for building up a sense of things in the old paper environment; and (b) the effectiveness of different kinds of computer assisted processing (for example the use of different algorithms) for automating the generation of a sense of things that could be taken as authentic, at least in the sense of matching the way those things had been experienced by those who were a part of them (Chandler, 2016).

Research of this kind is also starting to take place in a practice rather than an academic context. For example, The National Archives have recently experimented with the tools and techniques brought together and marketed as e-discovery software and have started to learn how and to what degree they can (and cannot) assist in, amongst other things, 'understanding born digital collections at a high level' and 'extracting meaning' (The National Archives, 2016, 14, 17). Experiments of this kind allow archivists to relearn how to work with the material remnants of an organization and the available processing power (now encompassing the use of algorithms, text mining and so on) to not just generate any sense, but a specifically archival sense. What this specifically archival sense entails is not very well defined, but it can perhaps be tentatively seen as being one which acts as an authentic or at least reasonably accurate representation of the activity from which it arose; a sense which would make at least some sense to those, like the staff members in Chandler's study, involved in that original activity.

Conclusion

This chapter started by recalling the argument made on several occasions that archival 'methods are out of sync with the problems by more than an order of magnitude' (Bearman, 1995, 382). It took the solutions that had been suggested to the problems of processing as its starting point, not to provide more solutions, but rather to consider the framings and meanings of archival processing implied by those solutions.

In this way, consideration of David Bearman's suggestion that 'archivists will need to identify that information which can be obtained from outside, and import it into their systems automatically' led to a conception of archival processing in terms of the process of moving information across different systems (Bearman, 1989). Then again, consideration of the suggestion that 'archives should not describe records, but, rather, document records-creating activity' led to a conception of archival processing in terms of the process of keeping track of and recording information about a large number of different sorts of entities and the relationships between them (Bearman, 1995, 401). In both cases, another framing was highlighted, which distinguished between manual and automatic processing and between the need to communicate information in a way that made that information available for processing by both human and computer agents. This ultimately led to one more framing of archival processing, this time in terms of the process of information processing.

One of the purposes of this chapter was to highlight the way in which, by defining archival processing solutions in certain terms, we also frame both archival processing and the problems its faces. If we are to realise different futures for archival processing, we will need to be alert to such framings and be able to move beyond them. For example, being alert to the framing of moving information across different systems can lead us to question the boundaries we choose to place around those systems and whether we are taking a broader or a narrower view of them. Then again, a framing of keeping track of and recording information about many different sorts of entities and the relationships between them, can lead us to a renewed recognition that the magnitude of the task we set ourselves is indeed truly immense.

The final re-framing, in terms of information processing, perhaps allows for the possibility of a solution, this time in terms of an answer to the question: how can we combine the computer's information processing, admittedly faster and more accurate as it is over large quantities of digital material, with our own sense-making? David Bearman framed the processes 'of analysing the records themselves in order to find clues to context, and then entering this data into our own descriptive systems by keyboard' as 'costly and inefficient steps'

(Bearman, 1989). It may well be that, with tools like DROID, we are rapidly removing the need for the last of those steps. However, the first step is, to my mind at least, not one we should eradicate, but a skill we should celebrate and develop. Relearning this skill in respect of the new material we deal with, and the new tools and vastly increased processing power available to us, is the future of archival processing.

References

Bearman, D. (1989) *Archival Methods: Archives and Museum Informatics Technical Report #9*, Archives and Museums Informatics, www.archimuse.com/publishing/archival_methods.

Bearman, D. (1992) Documenting Documentation, *Archivaria*, **34**, 33–49.

Bearman, D. (1993) Record-Keeping Systems, *Archivaria*, **36**, 16–36.

Bearman, D. (1995) Archival Strategies, *American Archivist*, **58** (4), 380–413.

Chandler, K. (2016) *Exploring the Principle of Provenance with Social Network Analysis*, Masters of Archival Studies Thesis, University of British Columbia.

Chandler, K. (2017) Investigating original order with Cybernetics and Community Detection Algorithms, *Archival Science*, **17** (3), 267–83.

Duff, W. and Harris, V. (2002) Stories and Names: archival description as narrating records and constructing meanings, *Archival Science*, **2** (3), 263–85.

Evans, J. (2007) *Building Capacities for Sustainable Recordkeeping Metadata Interoperability*, PhD Thesis, Monash University.

Greene, M. and Meissner, D. (2005) More Product, Less Process: revamping traditional archival processing, *American Archivist*, **68** (2), 208–63.

International Council on Archives Experts Group on Archival Description (2016) *Records in Contexts: a conceptual model for archival description*, Consultation Draft v0.1, www.ica.org/sites/default/files/RiC-CM-0.1.pdf.

ISO 23081-2:2009 *Information and documentation – Records Management Processes – Metadata for Records – Part 2: Conceptual and implementation issues*, International Standards Organization.

Meehan, J. (2009) Making the Leap from Parts to Whole: evidence and inference in archival arrangement and description, *American Archivist*, **72** (1), 72–90.

Oxford English Dictionary (2018) Oxford University Press, http://www.oed.com/.

Society of American Archivists (n.d.) *A Glossary of Archival and Records Terminology*, www2.archivists.org/glossary.

Stanley, L. (2017) Archival Methodology Inside the Black Box: noise in the archive! In Moore, N., Salter, A., Stanley, L. and Tamboukou, M., *The Archive Project: archival research in the social sciences*, Routledge.

The National Archives (2016) *The Application of Technology-Assisted Review to Born-Digital Records Transfer, Inquiries and Beyond*, research report, www.nationalarchives.gov.uk/documents/technology-assisted-review-to-born-digital-records-transfer.pdf.

6

Access technologies for the disruptive digital archive

Sonia Ranade

Introduction

As archivists, we are in the business of the past. Since the advent of the digitally enabled office in the 1980s, that past is digital. Although we still talk in terms of creating 'documents' or 'files', the digital records we archive today are fundamentally different to their paper equivalents. Every step, from their original creation and use to their eventual archiving and preservation, has required new thinking, process and technology. Despite this, archivists have not significantly changed our approach to providing access to this material; our 'first generation' of digital archival catalogues still applies models originally developed for physical files.

In recent years, there has been much discussion of the challenges of accommodating the diversity, volume and richness of digital collections (see, for example, Johnson et al., 2014) and a new body of *digital* archival theory and practice is emerging. But whilst we grapple with these challenges we must remember that the shift to digital offers great potential too. If we can recognise that the essence of a digital record is data, which can be not only read but described, discovered and delivered with the assistance of digital technology, then the growth of digital archives opens up a wealth of new possibilities for access and use. The shift to digital is not a threat, but a real opportunity for the archival profession to re-examine our assumptions, embrace relevant technologies and re-invent what it means to provide access to digital archives.

The past is digital

Diversity

At The National Archives, our earliest digital accessions, dating from the start of the new millennium[1], include office documents, a virtual reality model, websites and executable computer code.[2] This diversity has continued to grow. We already hold records in over a hundred different digital formats and we expect this to expand rapidly (The National Archives, 2017). None of these digital files are directly human-readable but must be processed and interpreted with the assistance of computational tools. Some may be rendered and made viewable, others exist only as abstract data which we can manipulate and re-purpose, but not directly consume. Alongside this proliferation of formats, digital records often lack a cohesive structure, although formats such as datasets can offer pockets of order within the 'digital heap'.

We cannot provide meaningful access to this diversity via a single, standardised interface – for example, email collections lose much of their functionality when messages are presented as individual records – but neither can archives sustain a multiplicity of access routes, tailored to each individual format. We need a range of strategies to make the archive as exploitable as possible: from enriching records to make them discoverable, to surfacing our content via external tools and services.

Volume

Early digital records represented only a small addition to our traditional collections. Although they were different to paper, it would have been unwarranted to redesign archival practice around them. Understandably, the first generation of digital archives were collected, described and presented in much the same way as paper files. Since then, digital records have accrued in a steady stream. At the time of writing, The National Archives holds 700Tb of digital records, with as much again now due for transfer. The rate of accrual is unprecedented; the administrative records of a single inquiry[3] stretch to over one hundred thousand digital pages, while the records of a recent inquest[4] include 18Tb of audio-visual material – and our capacity to generate data continues to grow.[5]

At the same time, patterns of use have changed. Remote access to The National Archives' digital resources now exceeds on-site use of physical records by a factor of more than three hundred to one. It is clear that digital records are no longer merely an extension of our physical collections and cannot be treated as such. But these extraordinary volumes make both discovery and delivery difficult. How can the user find an item of interest among so many? How can the archive provide access to high resolution formats when a single 1-hour documentary film can occupy 300Gb?[6] A new, disruptive, second generation of digital archives will emerge to address these challenges.

In parallel with growing volumes, we have seen a shift in the nature of the archival file, to the point where it is debatable whether the concept of a file holds meaning for born-digital records. We must now manage and provide access at different levels of granularity, from entire collections down to individual objects. Digital records offer no easy equivalent to the standardised unit of production in the form of an archival box of records, neatly bound within a physical file cover.

Our approach to archival description does not fit the digital world either. It has become unsustainable for archivists and records creators alike to create an authoritative, high-quality description for each object and so the digital record may initially appear to be less rich and less discoverable than its paper equivalent.

Richness

Although digital collections often lack the richness of description and contextualisation that we create for traditional archival resources, in their native form digital records can be very much richer than we recognise. A digital photograph taken today will have a wealth of information embedded within it, often including a timestamp and geo-reference indicating precisely when and where the image was captured.[7] Similarly, in the corporate domain, recordkeeping systems can manage multiple versions of documents, tightly coupled to their audit trail, notes, indexing, classification, workflow and filing structure, along with cross references to related information – all of which contribute to making the record findable, meaningful and trustworthy in its original environment.

Records transfer processes typically collect only a superficial layer of this material, effectively reducing the multi-faceted record to a digital facsimile of a paper document. This is largely for ease of export; many corporate information systems do not export rich content by default, if at all. For the archivist, this simplification eases the accession of digital records, allowing us to squeeze them through our existing processes for archiving paper, even as it strips them of their inherent richness. Archiving a broader and deeper record will require us to re-think our approach to collection and exposing more of its richness will mean re-inventing what it means to provide access.

Archives as data

The diversity, volume and richness of digital records has tested our current collection and access model to its limits. But digital does not only bring challenges, it offers new opportunities too. Much of the data we handle is textual data and, fortunately, this is highly amenable to computational processing. These techniques may be applied to create new routes for discovery, presentation and use through re-building some of the context that is lost when digital records are transferred.

For born-digital material, the traditional catalogue is only one of many sources of information about archival records. Digital archival data also lies in the content of documents, both born-digital and digitised; in metadata provided by records creators and metadata extracted directly from digital objects; in links between records and links to external collections that can connect and contextualise them; in the data that users contribute; and in the data they generate as they use the archive. And there are further layers of information in the inferences we can draw by following links and in our understanding of data quality, uncertainty and confidence. It is clear that the archival catalogue alone cannot meet our needs for access. We will need to embed the catalogue into a much richer knowledge base that connects and exploits all these sources of information.

The essence of a digital collection is data, but this data will become a living, usable digital archive only through improved processes for *enrichment* and *contextualisation* (making records machine-processable and drawing them together), *discovery* (enabling users to find what we have) and *presentation and use* (enabling users to both 'read' and 'machine read' the archive). A range of technologies can be leveraged to support us in this work.

Enrich and contextualise

Recognising that digital archives are also data opens up the potential to compute over archival collections. Users of digital archives will want to apply computational techniques to work with records at scale and explore new types of research questions. To enable this, we, as digital archivists, must ourselves compute over the archive, making it machine-readable and enhancing access through linking and contextualisation.

A commonly applied approach to augmenting archival description is to enlist the support of volunteers. Early projects involved close co-ordination of on-site volunteers while more recent crowdsourcing approaches, built on mature platforms[8], have opened this up to even casual visitors. Content enrichment can take different forms, including transcription, indexing or tagging, annotation, contributing personal histories[9] and uploading related material.

Much of this activity depends on human insight but many enrichment tasks may be wholly or partially automated to deliver high-quality results at scale.

Enriching content

Since the primary source of non-textual archival data is images, much automated enrichment relies on image processing technologies. Within archives, the most widely applied technique is optical character recognition (OCR) for transcription of images of typed or printed documents. Handwritten text recognition (HTR) is a greater challenge but this is an active field of research and new platforms are helping HTR gain traction for manuscript transcription.[10] Both approaches can be used in combination with manual effort: a positive feedback loop, reviewing results at each stage and adjusting parameters or supplying corrections will improve accuracy whilst also providing a more satisfying experience for volunteers.

Similar techniques exist for speech. Developed for capturing voicemail messages in a business context, they can be applied to create transcripts which allow users to find interesting content within a longer recording. Advances have also been made in recognition of text or captions that appear in video images.

Applications of image processing for non-textual collections include morphological analysis of the imaged page to determine its structure. This can identify different types of page within a collection, locate features of interest (such as annotations) and offer precise, large-scale redaction of sensitive documents. Image analysis technology has obvious applications for search[11] and could also assist with tagging and indexing content that would otherwise be opaque to discovery – although training the models to work with archival content will not be a trivial task.

These deep learning applications are likely to benefit from a collaborative approach. Where individual institutions would struggle to produce sufficient training data, the archives sector as a whole may prove to be greater than the sum of its parts.

Enriching context

Under the archival principle of *respect des fonds* (grouping collections of archival records according to the entity by which they were created or from which they were received), the meaning we attach to records stems from our understanding of the functions that created them. But this is not the only way in which archival records may be contextualised. Our understanding of the circumstances of creation may be enhanced by setting records in the context of related material from both within and beyond the archive. This is an essential element of giving digital archives meaning and is vital if we are to facilitate cross-collection research in public archives that increasingly reflect cross-organizational ways of working.

Digital collections may be processed computationally to make connections. For example, a government record might be contextualised by links to news content in the days leading to the record's creation, legislation which arose from it, contemporaneous material published on the creating body's website and related material held in other repositories. Links such as these can augment archival description about the structure and functions of creating bodies, spanning institutional boundaries to re-connect distributed digital archives and aiding both the discoverability of collections and the ease with which researchers can understand what the records are and where they came from.

Digitisation

A wide range of enrichment techniques, including those described here, will transform our understanding of what it means to digitise a record. Once we recognise that high-quality digitisation can enable both reading and machine-reading, it will no longer seem adequate simply to create pictures of documents for remote access. The enrichment processes described here can make digitised material (and audiovisual collections) as usable and discoverable as born-digital textual documents, potentially enabling researchers to compute over the digital archive in its entirety. For this reason, in the text that follows, no distinction will be made between born-digital and digitised archival records.

Just as physical archives routinely invest effort in cataloguing, computing over records for enrichment and contextualisation will become a standard process for digital archives, seen as an integral element of making the digital archive re-usable by the widest cross-section of researchers.

Confidence and trust

Probabilistic data

Several approaches for automated processing of digital records have been identified here, many of which have improved greatly in recent years. Despite this, machine generated data is often felt to be of insufficient quality for archival description. For example, The National Archives uses OCR transcripts to support indexing and retrieval but does not make the OCR text directly available to users. Concerns about data quality arise, in large part, from a tradition of high-quality, curated archival description and the ensuing risk that messy, automated transcriptions will undermine confidence in the catalogue and, by extension, the institution.

Current approaches to archival description (International Council on Archives, 2011 & 2016) are limited to making authoritative assertions. Archives have not yet developed a practice of qualifying those assertions with an indication of confidence or an attribution of the source (whether human or software agent) or the date the assertion was made. The archivist's interest in provenance traditionally begins and ends with the *record* but in the digital sphere, the distinction between record, description and context is blurred.

When machine-processing archival content, we must be careful not to dismiss imperfect results. Descriptions curated by archivists are not immune to error and much of our existing catalogue data is already probabilistic in nature. For example, an examination of dates of birth in catalogue entries for a series of digitised Second World War service records[12] shows one individual who was born after the end of the war and several more who would have been infants at the time. But the presence of error does not mean the data lacks value. There are structures and patterns in errors and omissions which can be understood and exploited using statistical techniques. A missing date of birth might be modelled by a probability distribution generated from the dates of birth of the cohort in question. This type of distribution bears little resemblance to an entry in a 'date of birth' field in an archival catalogue, but for automated processing of the records it has real utility and is greatly preferable to missing data. Our future 'archival knowledge base' should be able to accommodate statistical modelling of this kind.

We must also be able to accommodate different, perhaps conflicting, interpretations of the records. For example, crowdsourcing may generate multiple descriptions for a single record if it is indexed by several contributors. Our instinct as archivists (and the limitations of our current archival catalogue structures) prompt us to process this raw data into a single 'consensus' view that resembles a catalogue description. We must develop a descriptive practice that would support presentation of the raw data with its multiple perspectives and *also* allow us to offer our derived data, suitably qualified with the confidence measures which constitute an essential component of such data.

Mathematical probability provides good ways of expressing uncertainty and The National Archives has learnt some valuable lessons from the *Traces Through Time* research project (Ranade, 2016).

We will need to further develop quantitative methods to deal with risk and uncertainty and our understanding of both will evolve as we gather more information and make more connections. An iterative, Bayesian approach is likely to prove useful, allowing us to make a start despite our limited knowledge and to refine our understanding as we gain experience. In parallel, we will need to explore how to expose the workings of the models to users who lack a prior understanding of statistical methods. We might envisage a service that would enable researchers to explore and adjust the models and confidence thresholds to fit their own research questions.

Trust

We have seen that when we stop treating digital records like paper and start to understand that they are data, this creates routes for users to combine and re-purpose records in new ways to create new resources. One of the chief concerns about this is the issue of trust. If our records are separated from the archival structures that bound and contain them, how will users understand what they are looking at and where it came from? This is a valid concern but, as with the access issues we have already considered, the digital medium may offer us more opportunities than threats.

Digital objects are a stream of ones and zeroes that can be processed to create a hash – like a 'signature' which is unique[13] to that object. Creating such hashes is well established practice for digital archives and provides assurance that the object has not changed or become corrupt. Publishing the hash would offer our users the same assurance. At any time, a copy of a digital record could be verified simply by generating a hash and comparing it with that published by the archive. Provided that the hashing algorithm is sufficiently robust, this addresses the risk of forgery or alteration after a record is released from the control of the archival environment. But what about the integrity of the archive itself? A mechanism such as a distributed ledger could be used to prevent the archive (deliberately or otherwise) changing the hash at a later date. This is particularly important for records that are closed for extended periods and for material behind a paywall where it is more likely that users will keep and share copies rather than obtaining them directly from the archive.

Records still held by the creating body lie outside this mechanism. As archivists we must also consider what we can do to build trust in information before it passes into our custody. The National Archives' *Digital Strategy* (2016) identifies the opportunity to provide benefit earlier in the process of creating a digital archive. It casts archivists not as passive collectors of historical material but in an active partnership with records creators, starting before a record is even created to advise on digital preservation issues when new systems are specified. This will, in turn, help archives deliver the capability to preserve and provide access to new types of records.

Once records have been archived, we can and should be more transparent about what happens to them. In this new environment, where records can be freely repurposed, transparency will replace control as a mechanism for building trust. Archives will have to provide better information about processes for the capture and preservation of the digital records with which we are entrusted. When we enrich descriptions, arrange records, take preservation action or hold multiple, perhaps format-shifted, versions, we will need ways to make that evident to users.

Material that is released from the archive may be re-purposed or combined with other sources to create new data. This was also true of information from our physical collections, which could only be related back to the original archival source by means of robust referencing. Digital records have the benefit of being citeable to a lower level of granularity: down to the individual digital object, not just the archival file. Textual content within an object may also be traceable back to the archive. Sorokina et al. (2006) find that pairs of documents where four sentences share a 7-gram (seven-word phrase) are unlikely to be independently created texts. Assuming, firstly, that re-use will focus on text with meaningful information content, rather than boilerplate text, and, secondly, that we will open up the contents of the archive for computational processing, it should be possible to locate the archival source of re-purposed material with some degree of confidence. Commercial technology developed for plagiarism detection[14] can be applied in this context to evaluate the degree to which two texts overlap and to understand the probability that they share a common source.

A combination of these technical approaches will support us in freeing archival content for new and innovative use, while keeping it connected to the archive and firmly anchored in an environment that supplies identity, context, provenance and trust.

Discovery, presentation and use

We regard archive users as 'our users' or 'our audience' but it is important to remember that they are not ours, at least, not exclusively. Nicholas and Clark observe that users 'bounce around the digital domain', moving freely between services (Nicholas and Clark, 2015, 23). These users make little distinction between archive, library and museum collections as they select and recombine material from different sources. In this environment, it is unrealistic to expect users to learn about archives before they can engage with and benefit from our services. We also need to recognise varied levels of user motivation: from users who know (more or less) what they seek, to those who may not even know what an archive is but simply wish to understand what we offer.

Access services must rise to these challenges. We must provide access for both reading and machine-reading; accommodate the rich and diverse nature of the records themselves; and offer content, context and description that are generated automatically or contributed by users (as well as curated by archivists and records creators). In addition, the potential for ongoing processing means that the presentation of digital records and their descriptions need not be 'frozen' at the point of accession. The archival profession is still exploring what it means to offer a continually evolving contextual understanding of digital records.

We will need to develop coherent access models which offer the flexibility to meet the needs of a diverse audience, alongside sufficient gradation to control access to material with different sensitivities and risks.

Discovery

The most familiar means of locating information within an archival collection is search. The web has provided a *de facto* standard for the search interface in the form of the single search box that takes words or a phrase and returns ranked, relevant hits, topped with additional content judged to be of particular relevance. In the commercial world this content might be driven by advertising, while for archives it may be used to prioritise relevant research guides or audience-specific 'landing pages'. In developing new interfaces for search, we would need to be sure that the benefits of deviating from this familiar model outweigh the additional cognitive burden on users. But that does not mean that we should implement search without intelligence – the simplicity of the interface means we must do the work so our users don't have to.

The task of retrieving interesting information in response to a query is much more than simply submitting keywords to an index and returning matching results. The choice of underlying search technology is important, but archives must apply it with an awareness of the content and structure of our collections and we must develop a deeper understanding of our users' needs. An obvious complexity of searching over digital archives is the diversity of the data. Search technologies are emerging that will scale and flex to accommodate this diverse and unstructured content.[15] These could be coupled with assistive interfaces in the form of 'bots'[16] that provide mediated access (Pugh, 2016).

Alternatives to search and browse have emerged in the form of exhibition-style content, designed to help users understand what the archive might contain.[17] This can be highly engaging but typically exposes only a tiny fraction of the collection and requires a level of curation that is unsustainable for most institutions. Computational approaches to offering exploratory access, based on automatic classification, or topic modelling[18] could help address this.

Machine classification has been extensively trialled for allocating content to pre-defined taxonomies, however, more fluid organization is also possible (Saleiro et al., 2016). Categories can be generated directly from the content to synthesise clusters of records which cut across archival arrangement, enabling thematic access and connecting with external resources. For example, a simple entity analysis of catalogue records in The National Archives' *Discovery* will reveal several thousand records containing the word 'penguin', from 45 different archives. Semantic analysis might reveal that these belong to larger clusters of records including 'birds', 'publishers' and 'ships'.

The largest groupings (which are not necessarily the most generic) could serve as 'hubs' supporting further exploration and allowing users to drill down into the content.

The term 'explore' is used here to represent a mode of access that is distinct from 'browsing' via the hierarchical arrangement of the catalogue. These additional routes for navigation need not replace the current structures but can enhance them for a wider audience.

A concept which balances these two extremes of 'search' and 'explore' is serendipitous search, which attempts to offer results which are both relevant and unexpected. For example, hits for a search on 'oil spills' might retrieve images of penguins wearing sweaters (Bordino et al., 2013). In this model, instead of prioritising similar material, the ranking algorithm tries to present a diverse cross-section of the retrieved material in the hope of catching the user's interest or returning a hit that the user perhaps did not know they were interested in.

Present and enable use

In dealing with digital records, archives have so far focused on the immediate challenge of volume. As we start to address this, the ergonomic challenge will come to the fore. For those records that are still consumed by reading, a limitation of the digital medium is its lack of tactile feedback. There have been various efforts to address this, from interfaces that re-create the physical record office environment[19], to augmented reality models that overlay information from multiple sources, and even the development of a haptic sofa to support a truly immersive experience (Alam et al., 2011).

However, as we have seen, digital records are not simply format-shifted paper and it is not always clear what it means to present the record itself. For example, how should we provide access to a work of digital art? Or to records with a strong temporal dependency? In these cases, we need to provide access not to a record, but to an experience. Our new access models will need to be temporally and contextually aware, enabling the reader to explore content through the lenses of time, place and identity.

The record may not be renderable at all. For example, what would it mean to look at a neural network?[20] Do we really want to 'read' a seismic dataset? Thinking back to The National Archives' executable file from the turn of the millennium, it is currently presented as a set of screenshots allowing the researcher to form an impression of the original user experience, but not to recreate the working of the system. In the future, we might provide access by emulating the original operating environment to enable the researcher to interact with the record. At the very least, we could deliver the original digital objects for users to take away and work with outside the archive.

In the near future, the majority of visitors to archives will still want highly mediated access to the collections. However, a growing number of users wish to work with archives in a data-centric way, taking aggregations of digital records away to work with at scale, to identify patterns and allow different stories to emerge. We can imagine a continuum of services: from access to individual documents for reading, to the provision of services and infrastructure for querying and computation, to the supply of data for re-use outside the boundaries of the archive. We will need to build services that let users choose and export data or offer access to rich content via an API.

We might regard the API as the 'default' interface, with other services built on top of this. These services could include an archival catalogue or inventory but could equally be built by third parties (perhaps on a commercial basis) to provide tailored access to particular records or to create virtual collections drawn from different institutions. This model could start to address the sustainability issues in developing specialised interfaces for individual records series or in providing more highly mediated services for particular audiences.

Conclusion: the future is digital

The future digital archive is diverse and rich and is wider and deeper than traditional records collections. An archival catalogue, essentially designed as a descriptive inventory of paper files, will no longer serve us if we are to provide meaningful access to digital archives. Instead, we must embrace a range of disruptive technologies to build and provide access to an interconnected knowledge-base about our records. Of course, there is nothing to prevent us also generating a descriptive inventory of our digital records if we wish to do so!

Achieving this transformation in access relies on us overcoming two challenges: we will need the skills to identify, adapt and deploy new technology and we will need to recognise that technology is only an enabler. Unless we also change our thinking and practice to become instinctively digital archivists, we will bear all the additional risk, complexity and cost that arises from the shift to digital, without reaping any of the rewards.

Addressing the technical challenges will require greater collaboration across the archives sector, with other collecting disciplines and between archivists and digital professionals. In addition to a continued emphasis on trust and context, four clear themes have emerged from The National Archives' early exploration of technology for a second generation digital archive:

- **A focus on users as both consumers and contributors of content**: we must do more to understand user motivation and expectations and create services that are engaging and intuitive, with user research recognised as a core element of service development.
- **A sustainable, 'digital first' approach**: applying automated, large-scale processing where possible, before we turn to resource-intensive, manual approaches. Our aim is not to replace the skill or insight of specialists but to invest their effort carefully and to greatest effect.
- **A more intelligent use of technology**: adapting and tuning technology developed for other applications to the archival environment. As we do this, we must think less in terms of tools and systems and more in terms of shared platforms and commodity services, investing engineering effort (where appropriate) to share not only our knowledge of useful approaches but to make these available across the archives sector and the wider galleries, libraries, archives and museums (GLAM) ecosystem.
- **An acceptance of messiness and uncertainty**: We cannot afford to create researched, curated archival metadata at scale and neither can we afford to lose the nuances in our messy data by cleansing it or imposing structure and order where they did not exist. We must recognise that much of our data is probabilistic in nature, be more transparent about uncertainty and adopt tools and approaches that embrace it.

The challenges faced by archivists require a significant shift in archival thinking, including a renewed emphasis on usability and transparency, which will take their place alongside trust and context as key features of a new access model. This shift is already underway and some innovative developments, which exploit the potential of the digital medium, have been highlighted here. Although there are many such examples, for the most part these exist as isolated services or small-scale pilots. The archival community has been slow to generalise from successful initiatives or to transition successful experiments into mainstream practice. Technical advances that can assist us with the task of enrichment, discovery and delivery of digital archives are emerging all the time. The limiting factor in transforming access to archives is not the availability of tools, computational power or storage. We are limited only by our collective imagination.

The future digital archive will be diverse and multi-faceted, contextualised within a fluid network of resources which is augmented over time to support ever new lines of research and enquiry. If we are to release the potential of these digital collections, we must look beyond the archival catalogue to imagine and build the archival access services of the future.

Notes

1   For The National Archives, the old millennium started in 1086 with the Domesday Book (TNA reference E 31). By the new millennium, digital records were being harvested at scale, for example, the snapshots of the Inland Revenue website in the UK Government Web Archive (TNA reference IR 153).

2   For example, *Virtual reality model created by the Formal Investigation into the Loss of the MV Derbyshire* (TNA reference MT 205/2/8). Inland Revenue executable file *Electronic tax return* (TNA reference IR 152).

3   *Records of the Inquiry into allegations of human rights abuse of Iraqi nationals by British troops in the aftermath of the battle of Danny Boy* (The Al-Sweady Inquiry). TNA reference ASI 2.

4   Audiovisual material from the *Hillsborough Independent Panel (Hillsborough Stadium disaster)*. TNA reference HO 519.

5   Described as 'The largest Big Data project in the Universe', the Square Kilometre Array will capture a terabyte of data per second

(www.skatelescope.org). Closer to home, the Internet of Things will create another step-change in the rate at which we create data: Intel predicts that a single self-driving car will generate 4Tb of data from just one hour's driving (www.networkworld.com/article/3147892/internet/one-autonomous-car-will-use-4000-gb-of-dataday.html). In cities, traffic lights, building management systems and a network of cameras will all generate public data which has the potential to be mined for current insight and future history. We need to think very hard about what to keep and for how long.

6   In addition to duration, the file size of video is determined by factors such as resolution, bit rate, the degree of lossy compression applied (this affects picture quality) and potentially by the image and motion complexity of the events depicted (sports action or similar high motion events being more difficult to capture and encode than 'talking heads' or scenes with minimal motion). The 300Gb RED-cinema video described could be delivered as high quality compressed MP4 at a hundredth of the size, but with some loss of these features. The extent to which users expect access to original vs presentation versions of digital records has yet to be fully explored.

7   For example, the Exchangeable Image File Format or EXIF (www.tinyurl.com/jeita-exif).

8   For example, *Operation War Diary* on Zooniverse (www.operationwardiary.org).

9   For example, *Memories from the Islands* on the UK Government Web Archive (www.tinyurl.com/ukgwa-memories-sewing).

10   *Transcribe Bentham* project (blogs.ucl.ac.uk/transcribe-bentham).

11   For example, Visual Search at www.cortexica.com/technology.

12   War Office, Home Guard records, Second World War (TNA reference HO 409).

13   *'First ever' SHA-1 hash collision calculated. All it took were five clever brains . . . and 6,610 years of processor time*, The Register, (www.theregister.co.uk/2017/02/23/google_first_sha1_collision).

14   For example, Computational Forensic Linguistics software (www.cflsoftware.com).

15   Elasticsearch (www.elastic.co/products/elasticsearch).

16   A *bot* may be defined as software that shares information via a service that is usually populated by humans.

17   Wellcome collection (next.wellcomecollection.org/explore).

18 *How do we do history in the age of computation and big data?*, The History
    Lab at Columbia University, www.history-lab.org.
19 *The Virtual Record Treasury* project (histories-humanities.tcd.ie/research/
    Beyond-2022).
20 www.wired.co.uk/article/ai-machine-learning-brain-scan.

References

Alam, K. M., Md Mahfujur Rahman, A. S. and El Saddik, A. (2011) HE-
    book: a prototype haptic interface for immersive e-book reading
    experience, *IEEE World Haptics Conference (WHC)*, Istanbul,
    ieeexplore.ieee.org/document/5945514.
Bordino, I., Mejova, Y. and Lalmas, M. (2013) Penguins in Sweaters, or
    Serendipitous Entity Search on User-generated Content, *ACM
    International Conference on Information and Knowledge Management*,
    https://research.yahoo.com/publications/6610/penguins-sweaters-or-
    serendipitous-entity-search-user-generated-content.
International Council on Archives (2011) *ISAD(G): General International
    Standard Archival Description*, 2nd edn, www.ica.org/en/isadg-general-
    international-standard-archival-description-second-edition.
International Council on Archives, EGAD – Expert Group on Archival
    Description (2016*) Records in Contexts – Conceptual Model*,
    www.ica.org/en/egad-ric-conceptual-model.
Johnson, V., Ranade, S. and Thomas, D. (2014) Size Matters: the
    implications of volume for the digital archive of tomorrow – a case study
    from the UK National Archives, *Records Management Journal*, **24**, (3) 224–
    37.
Nicholas, D. and Clark, D. (2015) Finding Stuff. In Moss, M. (ed.) *Is Digital
    Different?*, Facet Publishing, 19–34.
Pugh, J. (2016) Twitter Bots and AnneDroid Brontës, Workshop at *AHRC
    Common Ground*, York, June 2016.
Ranade, S. (2016) Traces through Time: a probabilistic approach to
    connected archival data. In *Proceedings of the 2016 IEEE International
    Conference on Big Data (Big Data)*, 3260–3265, 2016, Washington DC,
    ieeexplore.ieee.org/document/7840983.
Saleiro, P., Teixeira, J., Soares, C. and Oliveira, E. (2016) TimeMachine:
    Entity-Centric Search and Visualization of News Archives. In Ferro, N. et
    al. (eds) *Advances in Information Retrieval*, ECIR 2016, Lecture Notes in

Computer Science, 9626, Springer, Cham.

Sorokina, D., Gehrke, J., Warner, S. and Ginsparg, P. (2006) Plagiarism Detection in arXiv. In *ICDM '06 Proceedings of the Sixth International Conference on Data Mining*, 1070–1075, December 2006, Washington DC.

The National Archives (2016) *Digital Strategy*, www.nationalarchives.gov.uk/about/our-role/plans-policies-performance-and-projects/our-plans/digital-strategy.

The National Archives (2017) The PRONOM file format registry. A key resource for digital preservation, can characterise 1493 distinct file formats at the time of writing. New signatures are added regularly (www.nationalarchives.gov.uk/PRONOM).

Acknowledgements

With thanks to my colleagues Mark Bell, Alex Green, Ian Henderson and Anthea Seles who contributed many of the examples of innovative approaches highlighted here.

7

Multiple rights in records: the role of recordkeeping informatics

Barbara Reed, Gillian Oliver, Frank Upward and Joanne Evans

Introduction

The purpose of this chapter is to provide an introduction to a paradigm shift in ways of thinking about current recordkeeping environments. We begin by explaining recordkeeping informatics, a continuum-based approach to managing authoritative information in the ever shifting, complex and technologically challenging times that confront all of us, including organizations.

We then develop these ideas through a case study of recordkeeping requirements for those who as children experience out-of-home care as a result of child welfare and protection policies. Out-of-home care is the term used in Australia for 'the care of children and young people up to 18 years who are unable to live with their families, often due to child abuse and neglect. It involves the placement of a child or young person with alternate caregivers on a short- or long-term basis' (Australian Institute of Family Studies, 2015). These experiences place lifelong identity, memory and accountability needs on the governments and organizations providing these services. Our case study will explore the macro and micro challenges that arise for individuals, organizations, governments and societies as a demonstration of the utility of recordkeeping informatics in designing archival futures in which multiple rights in records are embedded.

Recordkeeping informatics

The development of recordkeeping informatics has been underway for the past eight years. The original motivation for this work was the need for an up-to-date textbook based on records continuum thinking to support teaching and learning for contemporary recordkeeping. The second edition of Jay Kennedy and Cherryl Schauder's *Records Management: a guide to corporate record keeping* (1998), is the only title currently in print to fit the bill, but its publication date means that the content, although still valid, is inevitably dated. During our first meeting to discuss the outline of an updated text, it became clear that it would not be possible to address contemporary recordkeeping requirements adequately within the constraints of what had developed as a discipline and occupation in the paper world.

The definition of informatics that we use explains the discipline as 'the science of information. It studies the representation, processing, and communication of information in natural and artificial systems. Since computers, individuals and organizations all process information, informatics has computational, cognitive and social aspects' (Fourman, 2003, 237–8). This definition emphasises that informatics is not just about technology but is inclusive of individuals and socially constructed entities also playing key roles. The definition also notes that 'informatics' can be used in combination with the name of a discipline, to denote 'the specialization of informatics to the management and processing of data, information and knowledge in the named discipline' (Fourman, 2003, 237). In this case, the discipline is recordkeeping; the systems, activities and processes needed for efficient and effective management of information for accountability and evidential purposes.

The main features of recordkeeping informatics are detailed in *Recordkeeping Informatics for a Networked Age*, a result of the eight years of writing and discussion of the concept (Upward et al., 2017), and are only briefly summarised here. A matrix consisting of two building blocks (continuum thinking and metadata) together with three facets for analysis (information culture, business processes and access) provides a framework encompassing the key areas for consideration.

Recordkeeping informatics is a sense-making approach, aimed at creating situational awareness of the complex, contested and dynamic environments in which recordkeeping takes place, to guide decision

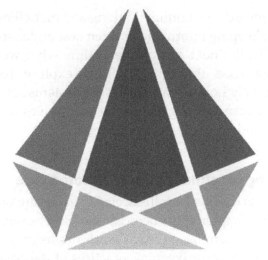

Figure 7.1 *The Recordkeeping Informatics Matrix*

making and systems design in order to identify and meet evidence, memory and accountability requirements. A long-standing theme in Australian records continuum literature has been that lifecycle models for institutionalising archives no longer work. Whether the processes relate to the formation of an archive within current recordkeeping activities or take place after a lapse of time, thought about the creation of the archive itself should precede predicting its management over spacetime.

A continuum-based informatics approach focuses attention on the point of creation across the breadth and diversity of the archival multiverse whether it relates to cultural heritage informatics, medical informatics, health informatics or any of the myriad of other prefixes that can be put in front of the word. All forms of informatics are dependent upon the quality of the archives they form, an argument that should be easy to present to others and when presented effectively will expand the breadth and depth of interest in archival formation processes across all disciplines and organizations. Recordkeeping informatics, as one specialisation within that breadth, can provide a model for the development of archival depth. No specialisation provides a more significant testing ground for the development of ethical approaches than an activity that can be so readily used for liberating or repressive purposes.

As with the records continuum thinking and modelling on which it is based, recordkeeping informatics is often best understood by seeing it performed. In the next section we outline what we believe is a compelling use case through which to explore recordkeeping informatics, namely how to ensure that the systems set up to protect children from abuse and neglect do not themselves cause harm – a recordkeeping and societal grand challenge.

Recordkeeping for childhood out-of-home care

The details of this complex, multi-faceted use case are outlined in the Appendix to this chapter. It has been chosen as an example for several reasons. It is a problem facing many countries as they grapple with the consequences of recordkeeping practices of the past and how to transform these practices into an alternative and more responsive future. As well as a number of inquiries in Australia over the past 20 years, Ireland, the UK, Scotland, Sweden, Canada, Norway, Iceland, Denmark and Germany have all investigated, or are investigating, the institutional abuse of children (Evans et al., 2015). It interfaces to issues of significant social concern, grappling with complexities in managing highly sensitive personal information. It highlights the very complex set of issues that must be considered when addressing significant change within organizations, both in terms of digital transformation and emerging individual rights to control information.

Our case study is fictional but seems to resonate with international audiences. We tested this case scenario in three European contexts and in our own Australian context over 2016–17. The problems faced by those who were, for reasons completely beyond their personal control, raised in out-of-home care provide a sharp focus for exploring approaches through the multiple lens of recordkeeping informatics. Each lens brings with it a new way of focusing on issues, revealing the complexity of the environment and the interplays with which any solution must grapple. Put together in new ways, they outline the scope and dimensions of changes that need to be taken into consideration before systemic change can occur. The recordkeeping informatics approach positions practical steps that may be taken in an organizational context firmly within a changing, complex social environment. The social and the organizational, the personal and the corporate, the legislative compliance and the emerging concepts of ethical recordkeeping are all surfaced using this approach to this particular set of circumstances.

The core of the recordkeeping informatics approach is to determine what perspectives a recordkeeping approach brings to the interdisciplinarity needed within organizations to effect change. Our assertion is that the parts of the analysis enabled by recordkeeping informatics are always going to be more complex than the whole (Latour et al., 2012) – the notion of simplexity, that it is only when you recognise the complexity that the agenda for action becomes clearer.

Building block: continuum thinking

Continuum thinking derives from our much longer tradition of Records Continuum theory and praxis. At a theoretical level it connects recordkeeping practice to currents of social thinking that have traditionally accompanied huge expansions of critical thought (Upward et al., 2011). Continuum thinking recognises that simplistic, linear certainties are not appropriate to the complexities of the contested, multi-technology, digital environment. Rather it positions records as a still point in a continuous flicker of movement, recognising change is a constant and that everything is in a state of becoming, interconnected and continuous. It moves away from thinking about certainties, asserting that the fundamental nature of movement and change will fuel a recurrence of specific instances of particular problems. In that environment, no one should seek definitive approaches, but should approach problems with a creative impulse to recognise broad patterns and seek to re-purpose older ways of approaching similar problems. It also recognises that all information disciplines (amongst others) are critically involved in addressing the issues of managing digital information from multiple convergent, but not identical, perspectives.

Our case study is clearly located in the present in a fictional society facing a huge social change around managing children at risk and how to best help and support those children through their situation, not only in the present, but for their lifelong struggles with identity, perception of self and links to family and community. These questions are much broader than a recordkeeping frame of reference. Such endeavours involve multiple disciplines and reflect a significant social change to the perception and management of children. The clear social shift in thinking about children's rights can be traced to the impact of the UN Convention in the Rights of the Child from 1989, itself an outcome of recognition of human rights violations in many parts of the world.

The case study is located within a not-for-profit grouping of advocates for change, CARIL (Children-in-care Access to Records and Information in Larasutia). The change they are after is fundamentally about recordkeeping. The advocates of CARIL are concerned with how children are recorded, represented and given access to the records of their out-of-home care experiences. They are challenging the way organizational records about children in this situation are created, organized, managed and pluralised. They are concerned not only with access to historical records for those who have experienced out-of-home care, but also to improve recordkeeping practices to ensure that children currently in out-of-home care systems do not have the same issues as those experienced by older Care Leavers.

The past and present co-exist in continuum fashion. A linear approach to the problems of recordkeeping only address instances of problems. The impact of records on people's lives isn't restricted to a particular moment in time, it reverberates throughout the life of an affected person and has also been shown to have intergenerational repercussions (Lewis, 2017). To effect real change, the current practices of recordkeeping need to coexist with improved practices for addressing the records of the past. These are what they are, but the recordkeeping processes that surround them need to reflect more sophisticated understandings of their role in people's lives as they seek to make sense of out-of-home care experiences.

Central to the concerns of CARIL are questions of ownership of the record. They assert that information about a person is the individual's personal information and should therefore belong to the individual. This challenges the notion of traditional ownership of information which resides with the service provider or the funder of out-of-home care services. CARIL is asserting that personal information is a right belonging to an individual. There is no formal legal position that clearly identifies any such right; however, the trend towards enabling more definition and control of actions involving personal information can be observed in privacy law and data protection regimes in Europe, while being consistently rebuffed by technology companies routinely re-using and re-selling personal information under potentially dodgy terms of service. This issue intersects a much broader debate about privacy, personal information and emerging rights.

At the same time, the multiple rights and responsibilities of different disciplines involved in the compilation of a record of care are revealed. Counsellors in Australia, for example, have asserted very strict professional privilege rights to information created while the client/counsellor contact is made (Cossins and Pilkinton, 1996). This professional right undoubtedly has the intent of protecting the privacy of the individual from external parties not related to the counselling process. The notion arose in relation to access to such information during court cases trying allegations of rape. But the implications of such privilege when broadened out to other circumstances can act as a barrier to individuals being able to access records about their own experience.

Continuum thinking does not seek to fix or find a specific answer to particular problems. Rather, it aims to position the reasoning about how to approach a specific instance within a broader context involving past, present, social, organizational and individual requirements, law and emerging thinking, all within a structured means of surfacing the tensions and complexities which need to be considered and positioned alongside conflicting requirements. Compromise and balance is often required in moving towards an achievable praxis in circumstances where accommodation of all requirements cannot be reached.

The move to consider more than one continuum reality involves using the multiplicity of continuum applications in the information space. It may be that a publishing continuum needs to be considered beside a records continuum and an information processing and information systems data continuum. There are intersections and richness to be found in considering multidisciplinary approaches to how to approach information problems. These are not exclusive models, rather a record-keeping perspective that can be applied to all of the other continuum models, and vice versa. This is indeed the richness of interdisciplinary approaches that do not diminish or reduce one another but allow differences to inform practice and creativity to thrive.

Facets of analysis: information culture

Recordkeeping informatics sees the site of implementation in terms of practical realities. At the moment, this largely means within an organizational context, acknowledging that the notion of organization is fluid and shifting with multiple organizations involved in delivering parts or aspects of services. This is certainly the reality of out-of-home care, which has been delivered by various institutions and organizations in society over time. It may be that a church organization, or a charity, provided the funding and staffing for out-of-home care. It may be that this was done with, or without, government oversight. At times it may be all the above. If we take Australia as an example, different state governments have adopted different legislation and different levels of control over the funding provided to a range of organizations providing out-of-home care. A single child may move between carers and institutions many times in their childhood.

Within Australia, this really very complex jurisdictional framework proves hugely problematic for a child. Their record of childhood is immediately fragmented and the opportunity for confusion in responsibilities both during and after their out-of-home care exper- iences is multiplied. Children who in later life reside in jurisdictions other than that in which their care was given, immediately find inconsistencies in approaching access to records. Records tend to represent an organizational view – what do organizations need to do to conduct their business, with that business being quite specifically defined in terms of answering for their conduct. In this view, the child tends to become a commodity to be reported upon. Recordkeeping in this sense becomes focused on the business transaction and the records relating to a child reflect the organizational view.

Different organizations involved in the complex chain of respon- sibilities will have individual information cultures which may vary widely. All will devise recordkeeping to reflect their individual information culture. As society's attitudes towards children change, so too do the expectations and requirements placed upon organiz- ations to account for their actions. Where organizations are left to themselves to govern their own operations, the recordkeeping culture may be limited to the information culture within that organization. Where oversight and formal agreements are entered into, as in cases where governments outsource the provision of placement and support services for children, those contractual obligations for recordkeeping may be more clearly defined by standards or expectations on how out-of-home care should be administered.

Nonetheless, in the myriad circumstances of regulation, record-keeping is focused on the 'business' of delivering care to children. The ultimate participant in this network of organizations providing services is the child themselves. Recordkeeping has only recently started focusing on the child in ways that call for meaningful partici-pation of children and young adults in the decision making that impacts on their lives. They also seek to ensure that 'adequate and appropriate information is conveyed to children and young people about their history, plans for their future, education, health and other important areas, as well as jurisdictional practices, policies and legislative requirements that relate to them' (Department of Families, Housing, Community Services and Indigenous Affairs, 2011).

When that shift of perspective is placed within organizations, recordkeeping changes to reflect and involve the child in the 'business' of out-of-home care. Understanding that the child is being recorded and being represented in the record brings a quite different perspective to the requirements of recordkeeping. This changed emphasis brings with it an understanding that the representations of the child in the record needs to be about more than the transactional. The child's views, their thoughts and their interactions with the various people involved in providing services must also be represented. Where a child is removed from a family, the record becomes one of the major mechanisms to document those relationships to individual family members, to the child's identity and to their cultural background.

This shift in understanding significantly impacts the nature of the information culture within organizations. The responsibility to accu-rately, collaboratively and openly document specific circumstances of a child's history become paramount. Recordkeeping becomes less a reflection of transactions and more a critical part of the identity of the child, relevant not just during episodes of out-of-home care, but throughout that individual's life. Recordkeeping practices such as the creation of 'life story' books which document key activities, relationships and achievements in a child's life have now become incorporated into practice, along with detailed genograms created to record familial and cultural connections (Humphreys and Kertesz, 2015). But criticisms are still made that these documents are largely created by carers or case workers rather than the children themselves, that the maintaining of such resources suffers in time-pressed circumstances and that they do not always accompany the child in their movement through multiple placements.

Using technology to transform what and how such records are created with, or on behalf of, the child is currently being explored through development of web-based apps, actively recording the child's wishes and experiences. Broadly speaking, there is agreement that such resources belong to the child from the time of their creation. But the long-term sustainability of such endeavours is not yet discussed or thought through. It is not sufficient to consider such records as the only record that is needed. The organizational recordkeeping view is valid for the purposes of administering out-of-home care environments. The child needs access to and rights in these organizational records too. They continue to contain the organizational interpretation of a child's experience and evidence how they have fulfilled the parental responsibilities mandated in child protection legislation.

Putting these complex pieces together in terms of an information culture operating in any particular out-of-home care environment is essential to understanding what options exist to improve recordkeeping, how to bring the child's involvement in active documentation of their wishes and experience and supporting long term life chances for the children affected. Studying information culture, which includes the concerns of external stakeholders and advocates such as CARIL, can position practice to determine what recordkeeping interventions can be most effective, at what layer of the complex environment, and how to ensure that positive information cultures are created and sustained.

Facets of analysis: business process analysis

Within specific organizations, the way activities are carried out critically affects the records which are, or which could be, created. Within recordkeeping informatics, we refer to records as cascading inscriptions, acknowledging that these occur in many places, but stressing that the ability to think of records as being part of a continuously moving cascade of documentation provides a new way of conceptualising context. This view stresses the context, and the linkage between documents which tends to be regarded as isolated reflections of actions, when filtered through technologies. Thinking of the connections, thinking of the relationships and the consequences of documenting these simultaneous multiple cascades provides a further lens to analysing recordkeeping practices of the past, present and future.

In the context of the case study, how we bundle those cascading transcriptions making up the record alters with perspectives. CARIL is advocating the centrality of the child, but also the child in cascades of relationships with others. The child then is the central focus and the core mechanism to bundle transcriptions. With the technological environment enabling new ways of presenting information, there can be multiple simultaneous ways of bundling transactions together to suit different purposes. The organizational view must be served to ensure the accountability and monitoring roles, but the child's view must also be available and central.

The notion of putting the child at the centre again changes the way business processes can be carried out. Active involvement in the creation of the record at all points where it relates to an individual, changes the framing of business processes. If a child knows about records as they are being created and is made an active participant, the notion of closing the record to the child becomes redundant and counterproductive. Of course, there are questions of ensuring age appropriate knowledge for children, but, in reality, as Care Leavers often remind us, when the experience is lived there is not much point pretending that children don't know.

Thinking in terms of the bundling of business processes also permits a different perspective on what constitutes an organization. In Weberian terms, an organization tends to be self-contained and self-governed. But if we think of organizations as bundles of transactions, perhaps with a similar concept to 'joined up services' or supply chain models, then documenting the activities becomes cross-organizational. Information systems may then really become 'architectures that define social relationships and organisational actions' (Aakhus et al., 2014, 1190). What would this do to recordkeeping? A joined-up recordkeeping system to which multiple organizational and individual actors contribute, all focused on a child, recognising multiple rights and responsibilities, becomes possible and perhaps capable of being realised utilising new technology opportunities.

At the same time, in the context of the case study, the technologies introduced in multiple (not joined-up) organizations are creating a veritable tsunami of documentation. Young Care Leavers talk of the nightmare of being confronted with thousands and thousands of pages of documentation, printed out into flat paper versions, which document their journey through the child protection system. This tsunami of digital communications is preventing meaningful interpretation – obscurity through plenty perhaps. Is this the only way?

Facets of analysis: access

Recordkeeping informatics revisits Anthony Gidden's powerful articulation of different needs within information – both as an allocative resource stressing the power of production within the ever-expanding continuum and as an authoritative resource which focuses on documentation as reliable evidence of action supporting space-time management, mutual associations and life-chances (Giddens, 1986). The case study illustrates quite clearly the importance of the authoritative perspective of information – the core of recordkeeping. Being able to access records which are authoritative, which represent the realities of the times and which can be brought forward into multiple future environments clearly illustrates what we mean by space-time management, mutual associations and life-chances. Records for those who experience out-of-home care become the means by which identity, connection, understanding and well-being are nurtured and, for those dealing with past childhood experiences, where healing can hopefully take place.

In contemporary organizations, the representation of authoritative information is not always brought to the fore. Rather, the more obvious allocative view of information is paramount. This view tends to diminish the importance of multiple roles and perspectives, privileging retrieval above all else. This is the 'Google search' notion: if only immediate access to everything is possible, all will be well. In reality, as we all know as avid Google users, the resources are filtered through complex invisible and tailored algorithms and we rarely look beyond the first page or two of the thousands of results. Thinking only in terms of allocative resources will comprehensively fail to meet the needs of people represented by CARIL.

For Care Leavers who are now adults, the question of access to records is pressing. To be denied records about a childhood which they have experienced is an affront. To have their case files read by others and then presented to them with huge redactions to protect the privacy of third parties is confronting and seems totally disrespectful. Mechanisms for determining who can see what fail to provide the child/person centric view and also fail to account to the person who is at the heart of the record. Multiple legislative instruments purport to provide avenues for improving access, but the experience of many is that the poor recordkeeping of the past combined with the reluctance to compassionately interpret the intent of the instruments permitting access, combined with what seems to be a very defensive and fearful attitude in a culture of blame, present Care Leavers with a most unsatisfactory result when trying to access records.

Building block: metadata

The final piece of the recordkeeping informatics approach is the core importance of metadata. In the digital world, metadata is all. Content, without the connectors to other parts of the cascading inscription, is meaningless because it is out of context. The connectors are the metadata. How we construct the bundles of information representing organizations, actions and processes are all reflected in metadata. The capability to provide granular access and rights to information of all kinds is in the metadata. And the ability to trace what has happened to information is in the metadata. This latter metadata is core to the recordkeeping part of informatics. The trail of action about who has done what, when and under what permissions is the guts of a recordkeeping approach to information. And it is as relevant to a specific data field in a database as it is to the management of a line of code or to a collection of information resources controlled by specific governance rules. Recordkeeping metadata can be a major disciplinary contribution to any and every discipline and circumstance.

Professionally, the ability to think about recordkeeping metadata needs to become more embedded in practice and agile in application. It is not about cataloguing content. It is about identifying where the data is currently being captured in technologies that allows verifiable assertions of authenticity and reliability to be made to capture contextual and transactional context.

Recordkeeping metadata can be viewed from a minute level or from a macro level. It can cascade through different scales of approach. Indeed, the metadata models that serve recordkeeping can be thought of as a fractal, recurring pattern which applies at any and every layer of aggregation, with different values associated to the same basic pattern of metadata.

All systems are built on metadata. The centrality of attention to recordkeeping metadata in the digital environment will be key to reflecting each and every facet of analysis and in enabling the expansion of records into different environments across different time periods. The continuum concept of perdurance – persistence and identity through time – is built into metadata components which link together to enable interpretation and contextualisation. Building systems that acknowledge change but find mechanisms to allow past, present and future to connect is the ultimate goal of recordkeeping informatics' focus on metadata. A vision that is unachievable in the ways in which recordkeeping metadata is conceived in current systems.

Conclusion

A recordkeeping informatics view permits a focusing of attention on particular aspects of analysis. The specifics of information culture, business process and access need to be read against a particular circumstance. This provides a way of broadening and positioning a recordkeeping analysis from which specific actions can then be devised and prioritised. The building blocks – those aspects that are core to any recordkeeping informatics approach and are the frame of reference brought to bear – are continuum thinking, along with the more micro and situated determination of recordkeeping metadata that is essential to the management of digital resources.

Brought together in a coherent and connected framework, the recordkeeping informatics approach permits exploration in new technological realms. New and constantly emerging technologies need to be incorporated into practice. The new tools and technologies will keep coming. Recordkeeping professionals need to be able to assess their capacity to support evidence, memory and accountability needs in and through time and space. This will enable them to identify and manage recordkeeping risks in their deployment and impact on future design to better incorporate recordkeeping requirements.

Recordkeeping informatics provides a roadmap for thinking about short and long-term management of authoritative information resources in a technology driven world where archiving takes place at the nanosecond of creation. Setting up repeatable patterns (or fractals) for sustainable recordkeeping is the goal of the endeavour. Surfacing and applying these patterns will become one measure of our disciplinary success in a world being increasingly flooded with information sludge. There is so much information but with what meaning and how sustainable, for whom and with what assurances of good management for the multiple participants in records?

We hope, perhaps optimistically, that recordkeeping informatics can do even more than that. Informatics is not merely tacked on to twentieth century ideas about recordkeeping processes. It is a way of addressing the technical, social and knowledge forming aspects of the archive in all its ethical manifestations. It provides a way of spreading an understanding of archives across the many forms of specialised informatics that are likely to develop in this century and which might need to be capable of working together if humanity is to form future archives that serve adequate forms of authoritative information resource management.

Our use of the case study focused attention on just one example of complexity of individual rights over time. The case study, using the facets and building blocks of recordkeeping informatics, revealed a richness and depth of discussion to surface different approaches and concerns from each angle of interpretation. Collectively, these create a rich and nuanced exploration of factors critical to recordkeeping that can then be persuasively brought to the table for discussion with other disciplinary colleagues and alongside the voices of those with the lived experience and expertise. No one profession or advocate rules in this complex, ever-changing technological world. But we need to focus on what we bring to interdisciplinary and transdisciplinary discussions. Recordkeeping informatics is a powerful tool to use as the disciplinary articulation of recordkeeping in today's information environment. It will guarantee we are part of ensuring that archives of the future can better represent and manage complex rights in records.

References

Aakhus, M., Agerfalk, P., Lyytinnen, K. and Te'eni, D. (2014) Symbolic Action Research in Information Systems: introduction to the special issue, *MIS Quarterly*, **38** (4), 1187–200.

Australian Institute of Family Studies (2015) Children in Care, *CFCA Resource Sheet*, www.aifs.gov.au/cfca/publications/children-care.

Cossins, A. and Pilkinton, R. (1996) Balancing the Scales: the case for the inadmissibility of counselling records in sexual assault trials, *UNSW Law Journal*, **19** (2), 222–67.

Department of Families Housing, Community Services and Indigenous Affairs (2011) *An Outline of National Standards for Out-of-Home Care*, Department of Social Services, www.dss.gov.au/our-responsibilities/families-and-children/publications-articles/an-outline-of-national-standards-for-out-of-home-care-2011.

Evans, J., McKemmish, S., Daniels, E. and McCarthy, G. (2015) Self-Determination and Archival Autonomy: advocating activism, *Archival Science*, **15** (4), 337–68.

Fourman, M. (2003) Informatics. In Feather, J. and Sturges, P. (eds) *International Encyclopedia of Information and Library Science*, 2nd edn, Routledge, 237–44 (Division of Informatics, University of Edinburgh, Informatics Research Report EDI-INF-RR-0139: www.inf.ed.ac.uk/publications/online/0139.pdf).

Giddens, A. (1986) *The Constitution of Society*, Polity Press in association with Blackwells.

Humphreys, C. and Kertesz, M. (2015) Making Records Meaningful: creating an identity resource for young people in care, *Australian Social Work*, **68**, (4), 497–514.

Kennedy, J. and Schauder, C. (1998) *Records Management: a guide to corporate record keeping*, 2nd edn, Longman.

Latour, B., Jensen, P., Venturini, T., Grauwin, S. and Boullier, D. (2012) The Whole is Always Smaller than its Parts: a digital test of Gabriel Tarde's Monads, *British Journal of Sociology*, **63**, (4), 590–615.

Lewis, A. (2017) *Records and Rights of the Child: report of focus discussions*, eScholarship Research Centre, The University of Melbourne, http://rights-records.it.monash.edu/wp-content/uploads/2017/02/2017-01-27-Records-Rights-of-the-Child-Final-Report.pdf.

Upward, F., McKemmish, S. and Reed, B. (2011) Archivists and Changing Social and Information Spaces: a continuum approach to recordkeeping

and archiving in online cultures, *Archivaria,* **72,** (Fall), 197–237.
Upward, F., Reed, B., Oliver, G. and Evans, J. (2017) *Recordkeeping Informatics for a Networked Age,* Monash University Publishing.

APPENDIX to Chapter 7

Recordkeeping informatics: recordkeeping for children in out-of-home care

Larasutia is, like other countries, facing real social concern over how to assist those children who are removed from their families for protection. The issues are current, but also Larasutia is recognising that the way it managed these children in the past, is, by today's standards, not acceptable. The harm caused, both inadvertent and also sometimes by neglect or lack of attention, has been revealed to be substantial, life-long, and often not addressed by individuals until considerable time has passed (as many as 33 years after the event where there has been sexual abuse).

Jen Stolen, Kate Advo and Ivor Surf are three survivors of such 'care' in Larasutia and are now advocates for children currently in care, as well as working closely to represent the community of people who have previously experienced out-of-home care. In particular, they are committed to working with children currently in care to ensure that they don't suffer the same silencing and continued impact of the violence that they themselves experienced.

Jen, Kate and Ivor are members of CARIL (Children-in-care Access to Records and Information in Larasutia). This strong advocacy group represents not only current children in out-of-home care, but also past Care Leavers. They act as advisors to a number of jurisdictional enquiries, with government bodies regulating out-of-home care and with providers of this type of care to improve practices for children. Recognising their work is unsustainable if not funded, CARIL has recently been given project support funding. You, Imar, have been appointed to support the work of Jen, Kate and Ivor to develop a proposal for a child-centric recordkeeping system.

A briefing paper has been prepared for you (see overleaf). The issues are really complex and intertwined. The briefing paper summarises current positions.

Each of these positions are part of CARIL's advocacy to various bodies. But they are all underpinned by the belief in ownership and rights over personal information, regardless of who records, holds or manages it.

Meanwhile, there are always issues coming to CARIL's attention for immediate action. The latest in a constant stream of things is news of a significant data breach in the care providers' network, leaving personal information of children in care and their carers out there.

Issue	CARIL's position
Problems with third party privacy rules in obtaining access to records of the past and present	An individual should be able to access all information about themselves – with no exception.
Vast volumes of email and electronic documents swamping requests for access to records of the present	Providing Care Leavers with too much, undifferentiated information, is almost as bad as not providing enough information – better, more sensitive approaches are needed.
Rights of correction (annotation) of the official record	Why should the Care Leaver have to do this? This is a burden. Particularly for many Care Leavers whose education was scant and neglected. The official record is often offensive and wrong. We are investigating alternative documentation models to allow more than annotation rights.
Ownership of the record/ information about personal history and family history	The information about an individual and his/her family is their personal information and should belong to them, not some government department or service provider.
Privileged access to records and information	We represent a community who have suffered considerable abuse, neglect and have often faced life-long problems because of this. We should be given access to everything as part of a process of remediating past practices.
Better recording of actions/incidents	We were the passive victims of a system in the past. We are committed to improving the systems of the present. We want the rights of the child recognised. We want the voice and wishes of the child to be recorded and heard. We want an end to judgemental comments on records.

8

The accidental archive

Michael Moss and David Thomas

Introduction

In the Chinese philosopher Zhuangzi's famous parable, Zhuang Zhou dreams he is a butterfly, only to awake to discover that he was a man, but he is left with the nagging doubt as to whether he was Zhuang Zhou who had dreamed he was a butterfly or if he was a butterfly dreaming he was a man (Giles, 1926, 47). Brewster Kahle dreamed he could archive the internet, but in this chapter we will argue that he will wake up one day to find that the internet has archived him. Far from being an object that is archived, we will argue that the internet is itself an archive, but one which does not conform to the rules of archiving as we know them. The chapter will further go on to demonstrate that, like the world in which men can wake up to find they are butterflies, the internet as archive has a unique ability to change the past as well as the present. Those of us who work in the field of memory institutions need to confront this new world in which the internet is not archived but is the archive, not by claiming that it is not but by exploring its properties and possibilities.

In 2011, the Cinque Port Scribes mounted *The Last Word* exhibition that toured five of the churches on Romney Marsh: 'using redundant books and calligraphy developed as part of a discussion of digital books and their impact on the printed book market and whether this may lead to printed books becoming as precious as the hand-written manuscripts they originally represented'.[1] Perhaps surprisingly it was not a lament but a paean of wonder at the potential of this new form of communication.

One piece made from beautifully scripted strips of paper was 'Els' Chrysalis' by Els Van Den Steen with the legend: 'Metamorphosis – to be reborn anew to live again'.[2] Beside it the artist had written poignantly: 'The metamorphosis of the printed book is taking place right now! And just like before, the written word is evolving into a new form . . . To achieve the decomposing effect of the printed book, I used a rifle and a shotgun . . . Will the new ebook be a beautiful butterfly?'

She is not alone on this journey. David Levy is a computer scientist turned calligrapher which made him aware, like Els Van Den Steen, that the computer was not just 'a very powerful calculating device', but 'a tool in the lineage of the quill, the pen, the printing press, and the typewriter'(Levy, 2011, preface). He went to work at Xerox Palo Alto Research Centre (PARC) when the PC was being developed: 'I was no longer afraid that computer work would contaminate calligraphy, but was instead hopeful that calligraphy might contaminate computers' (Levy, 2011, preface).

The internet as archive

For Els Van Den Steen's ebook we might substitute archive, not as a utilitarian warehouse for digital stuff, but as something sublime with extraordinary potential to challenge the way in which knowledge is constructed because, as David Weinberger (2011, 61) asserts, it scales indefinitely. Alexander Stille (2002, 330) declared enthusiastically: 'The ability to read publications from India, Kenya, Manila or Buenos Aires is a fabulous resource that genuinely makes the world much richer and more varied'. He likened the internet to Raphael's School of Athens: 'a grand international forum of intellectual exchange' (Stille, 2002, 330).

Andrew Hoskins, whose field is memory studies but who is alive to archival concerns, wrote:

Before the digital, the past was a rotting place. Its media yellowed, faded or flickered, susceptible to the obscuration of use and of age. . . . The passage of this decay time afforded value and made the past worthy of careful excavation, re-imagination and representation.

(Hoskins, 2013, 387)

We might describe 'decay time' as an opportunity for reflexion and reflexivity or the difference between the court of law and court of history (Moss and Thomas, 2017, 51–2), but then Hoskins rejoined:

> But today's archive is a medium in its own right, liberated 'from archival space into archival time' (Ernst, 2004, 52). The avalanche of post-scarcity culture and the databasing of the multitude challenges decay time. Suddenly, the faded and fading past of old school friends, former lovers and all that could and should have been forgotten are returned to a single connected present via Google, Flickr, Ebay, YouTube and Facebook.   (Hoskins, 2013, 387)

He is not alone in believing that the searchable content on the internet is one vast archive that demolishes at a stroke the distinction between time past and time present. Writing in the *London Review of Books*, William Davies (2017, 3) asserted: 'Twenty years on, it has become clear that the internet is less significant as a means of publishing than a means of archiving. . . . This massive quantity of information sits there, ready to be interpreted, if only something coherent can be extracted from the fog'. This after all is what data analytics companies do in trying to work out our preferences, which Negroponte (1991) predicted all those years ago when he proposed the 'Daily Me', news tailored for every individual's interests.

The archival impulse

An archival response might well be flat rejection. It is not a proper archive, it does not observe any archival practice or conventions; but this would be tantamount to an editor of a newspaper declaring that the 'Daily Me' is not news. It is. It may be disintermediated, because it is tailored exactly to an individual's preferences, but much of the content will in some shape or form be mediated. The interdisciplinary textual theorist David Greetham (quoted in Evans, 2010, 6–7) would counter by describing 'the archive [proper]' in terms of 'loss/gap/ garbage'. In his exploration of the 'poetics of archival exclusion' he argued that archives do not tell us a truth about ourselves or our histories; they, rather, construct idealised images of our supposed collective history'.

Long before the advent of the internet, scholars were questioning the objectivity of archival appraisal (which after all only preserved a sliver of records) and catalogues themselves (Harris, 2002). Pierre Nora, the French historian, identified the 'imperative of our epoch' – that is, 'not only to keep everything, to preserve every indicator of memory – even when we are not sure which memory is being indicated – but also to produce archives' (Nora, 1989, 14). It is this archival impulse that led victims of the holocaust to create a counter archive buried in milk churns in concentration camps in the hope they would be discovered and the truth be told (Kassow, 2007). Artists in Moscow under Brezhnev followed their example, frightened that an authoritarian and repressive state would destroy their work.[3] The internet feeds such an impulse, not simply through oversight, as the default is to keep rather than the wastepaper basket (Mayer-Schönberger, 2009, 2), but through active participation by posting to social media sites or creating one which, try as it might, an authoritarian state cannot constrain. As David Weinberger (2011, 59) put it: 'The Net retains everything we post on it – often out of context and sometimes against our will'.

Anna Reading at King's College London has explored this phenomena through the lens of the London bombings in 2005:

> Digital media technologies have not simply collapsed the event and its memory into one another, as, perhaps, it may seem at first sight. Rather, events are witnessed in time and people's mediated witnessing, including mobile witnessing of events is articulated, rearticulated and disarticulated through intersecting temporalities.   (Reading, 2011, 299)

In this new 'extended present', as the distinguished sociologist Helga Nowotny (1994, chapter 2) describes it, there is no escaping from the archival gaze that has indeed emerged from its cocoon wrapped in the protective coating of archival practice and transformed into a butterfly of unimagined reach and diversity. Els Van Den Steen and her fellow calligraphers in the depth of the English countryside have every right to pause and wonder at this strange evolution into a living being very different from Michel de Certeau's assertion that 'the archive in its canonical form represents, not 'the past' in an amorphous sense, but rather the deaths of all those who lived it' (quoted in Moore et al., 2017, 5). Such death is frighteningly portrayed in Travis Holland's powerful novel *The Archivist's Story* (2007) that describes the creation of a secret archive of the manuscripts of writers imprisoned and then executed in Lubyanka prison by Stalin. Such closure, as repressive regimes have discovered, becomes almost impossible on the internet where counter archives, which have multiplied in the wake of post-modernism, are alive and well and do not need to be hidden in milk churns.

The difficulties of archiving the internet

The internet, with all its liberating potential, presents archivists with severe difficulties, notably whether it is capable of being archived at all.

In 1996, Brewster Kahle began what was to become his mission in life – to provide universal access to knowledge – and he began by archiving the internet. When the Internet Archive began in 1996, there were just 30 million web pages; at the last count, the Internet Archive held 279 billion web pages.[4] In 2003, the idea of an internet archive became bureaucratised with the separate establishment of the International Internet Preservation Consortium whose members are mainly national libraries.[5] Most web archiving is done by the libraries, who capture websites within their own countries and rely on technology developed by the Internet Archive (Lepore, 2015).

The trouble is they simply cannot achieve Kahle's idealised vision 'to create the digital-age version of the Great Library of Alexandria', by providing 'universal access to knowledge' (Evangelista, 2012) for three reasons. First, the nature of the internet has changed and is constantly metamorphosing. Secondly, it is too big and elastic to be captured. Thirdly, we are all inside the internet and it is hard to imagine how such an all-embracing organism could be captured.

The changing nature of the internet has been recognised by those working in the field of media and memory studies. David Karpf of George Washington University said:

> The Internet is unique among Information and Communications
> Technologies (ICTs) specifically because the Internet of 2002 has
> important differences from the Internet of 2005, or 2009, or 2012. It is a
> suite of overlapping, interrelated technologies. The medium is
> simultaneously undergoing a social diffusion process and an ongoing
> series of code-based modifications.   (Karpf, 2012, 640)

The internet is both unstable and 'consists of billions of sub-networks'
(Weinberger, 2011, 58). Andrew Hoskins has argued that 'the Internet
can hardly be conceived of as a single medium and its transformations
are more staccato rather than smoothly evolutionary' (2014, 662).
Moreover, it is not a single entity, as many imagine. It is dependent on
inter-connected data farms scattered round the world which can yield
quite different results depending on where you launch a search. De
Geuzen, founded in 1996 to explore amongst other things narratives
of the archive, built The Global Anxiety Monitor:

> ... which evolved out of De Geuzen's interest in mediatized images and
> the way their context and meaning fluctuate in the ecology of the world
> wide web. Presented as a multi-screen installation, the work
> simultaneously juxtaposes live Google image searches in different
> languages. Querying anxiety buzzwords such as terrorism, conflict,
> financial crisis and climate change, each language delivers its own
> unique set of results. What is projected is a continuous pulse of visuals
> and metadata reflecting occasionally convergent and at times conflictual
> perspectives. By continually performing timed searches, it becomes
> evident that query is driven by cultural biases and fed by local concerns.
> The Global Anxiety Monitor does not archive or document these
> processes, but rather it is a means of exposing the various Google worlds
> we may occupy at any given moment.'[6]

All this makes archiving in any meaningful way something called 'the
internet' impossible and confirms our identity within it.

Inaccessible content on the internet

We can see this using the example of family history. In 1996, an
American woman, Cyndi Howells, published a one-page list of family

history websites online. It contained more than 1,250 links.[7] Cyndi continued to add links to her website and it now contains over 336,000, beginning with 'Acadian' and ending with 'Writing Your Family's History.'[8] However, family history has largely moved away from the situation in the early days when individual researchers would put up family history sites which were capable of being archived. Now, online family history is dominated by large companies which make money by buying copies of records from archives, bundling them with a range of ancillary services and selling these to subscribers (cleverly, some of the content they sell has been provided 'for free' by subscribers themselves). The largest of these by far is Ancestry.com. Figures for the most used family history websites compiled by *GenealogyInTime Magazine*, show that Ancestry totally dominates the field. The magazine estimates that the top ten websites have 342,000 daily visitors of whom 227,000 are to sites owned by Ancestry (i.e. the Ancestry.com, .au and .uk sites plus Find a Grave and Newspaper. com).[9] Such sites, which largely operate within paywalls, are off limits to the web archiving organizations.

The same thing has happened across the web. Large, companies run social media sites (Facebook, YouTube, Twitter, etc.) which provide the technology and platforms for user (subscriber)-created content. Although this is a radically different business model to the inter-mediated services of traditional archives, libraries and museums, the one thing they have in common is that they still privilege content, albeit algorithmically as De Geuzen has shown. These websites are outside the scope of the web archives, because they are private fiefdoms where the underlying code will never be in the public domain and is heavily protected by patents. As we will see, they are too large and complex to archive. The nature of such sites has changed over time, making them increasingly valuable resources in their own right for a whole range of subject areas.

To continue our genealogy theme, Facebook has now become a major source for family history. Thomas MacEntree of Geneabloggers said on 3 May 2017:

> More genealogists are becoming comfortable with Facebook and sharing
> family history stories and genealogy successes there. Our demographic
> has learned how to handle privacy issues and to focus on just genealogy

on the largest social media platform in the world. A huge growth in
Facebook groups related to genealogy means this is where queries and
lookups have moved. Any genealogy society that is not at least
managing a Facebook page or group is seriously short-sighted.'[10]

According to the professional genealogist Katherine R. Willson, there
were 11,200 English language family history and history related sites
on Facebook in June 2017.[11] This is just one example of the use of
Facebook to create what are in effect mutual trust-based associations.

Size and complexity issues

The second difficulty is that the internet is now much larger and much
more complex than it was in 1996. Andrew Hoskin, (2018, 3), in the
spirit of Els Van Den Steen and David Levy, described the history of
memory and media, starting with oral culture, moving through print
and then television and film and finally, digital. He talked of the
transformation in recording and archival technologies that were
publicly regenerative of the mass of individual memories of the nodal
events of the last century. However, he said:

> Today the historical process of collection and encapsulation and
> archiving has not reached completion and success but, rather, its own
> failure. For the internet is the technology that makes visible our inability
> to encompass everything, because it is the first medium that is actually
> bigger than us.   (Hoskins, 2018, 3)

Or, to put it bluntly, the internet is simply too big to archive in any
conventional sense. Like the universe, it is a gigantic organic graph.
The title of David Weinberger's book *Too Big to Know* (2011) makes this
abundantly clear and his amplification is daunting: 'the publicness of
the Net has now made a pragmatic truth unavoidable. What we have
in common is not knowledge about which we agree but a shared world
about which we always disagree' (Weinberger, 2011, 181–2). An
unforeseen consequence is the polarisation of opinion that is fed by
and feeds the internet. At one extreme there is the right wing,
exemplified by Donald Trump, and on the other the liberal left,
particularly the jurists, who clearly articulate the implications of our

inter-connected world. It is wishful thinking by archivists, such as Richard Cox, that somehow the genie can be put back in the bottle using outdated tools and methodologies (Cox, 2017).

The weaknesses of internet archiving

Even the existing internet archives appear to be struggling. Despite Brewster Kahle's enormous labour in creating his internet archive, there are serious issues, particularly with the software used to access it: the Wayback Machine. Harvard historian Jill Lepore wrote:

> The Wayback Machine is humongous, and getting humongouser. You can't search it the way you can search the Web, because it's too big and what's in there isn't sorted, or indexed, or catalogued in any of the many ways in which a paper archive is organized; it's not ordered in any way at all, except by URL and by date. To use it, all you can do is type in a URL, and choose the date for it that you'd like to look at. It's more like a phone book than like an archive. Also, it's riddled with errors.
>
> (Lepore, 2015)

We need to ask Lepore and for that matter Richard Cox, if any of this matters very much, except to those trying to find a place for themselves and their skills in the new paradigm. Moreover, we need to question whether all these catalogues and indexes were ever fit for purpose. Derek Keene, the urban historian, does not believe so:

> I also had the free run of the archive vault, so to speak – the store behind the central office – and that was a real eye-opener because when you can see a massive town archive like that, you just realise how many things there were that you simply wouldn't gather from a catalogue. . . . I'm afraid I tell everybody that I ever teach an archives class to, to go to the storeroom! It's so important to be able to get that sort of direct access if you possibly can, but archive structures these days tend to prevent you doing such things.   (Keene, 2008)

This is just what the internet does, it takes the user direct to a metaphorical storeroom. Users may not be able to browse bookshelves, but they can meander serendipitously. The shift to the semantic web and to linked data that is not 'too fussy about metadata' (Weinberger, 2011, 187) opens up exciting possibilities (Gray, 2015, 35–79). We may dislike some of the content in the storeroom and we may not find what we are after, but the same is true of physical archives.

The Twitter archive

The real living demonstration of the impossibility of archiving the internet comes from the strange case of the Twitter archive. In 2010, the US Library of Congress and the popular micro-blogging company Twitter announced an agreement providing the Library with a digital archive of all public tweets from March 2006 (when Twitter first launched) through to April 2010. Additionally, Twitter agreed to provide the Library all future public tweets on an ongoing basis. While some cynics complained that much of the Twitter archive was valueless, a 2014 analysis of published academic research utilising Twitter data revealed over 380 publications from a wide range of disciplines, including computer and information science, communication, economics, social and behavioural sciences and the humanities (Zimmer, 2015).

The Library, however, has struggled with the project ever since. This seems to be partly because Twitter is much larger now than it was in 2010, with 500 million tweets a day in 2015, compared with 50 million in 2010. Just acquiring Twitter's back catalogue in 2012 pretty much doubled the size of the Library's digital archive. And back in 2010 they did not have embedded media such as videos and photographs. In addition, there are frightening problems of providing access, dealing with privacy issues and deciding on whether there should be restrictions on what tweets can be accessed (Zimmer, 2015).

In 2013, the Library gave an update on progress. It described how difficult it would be for it to provide access to the collection and said that currently available technology for searching the archive would 'require an extensive infrastructure of hundreds if not thousands of servers. This is cost prohibitive and impractical for a public institution' (Osterberg, 2013). In 2017, we approached the Library for an update. They referred us back to the 2013 update and told us that:

The Twitter collection has not been opened to researchers, and, at this time, no date has been set for the collection to be opened. The Library has been working to index the collection and develop use policies. These processes and the resulting outcomes must balance the goal of having a useful collection with two realities – first, the size and dynamic nature of the Twitter platform, and second, the resource realities of a public institution.   (Library of Congress, 2017)

We are all part of the archive

As well as the complexity and size of the internet, there seems to be something else at play here. In the case of the internet, we are not archivists looking from the outside at a system we can archive; the convergence of communications with the archive has meant that we are all part of the archive (Hoskins, 2016). As David Weinberger explains, the concept of *namespaces* is testimony to why this is the case:

> The namespace approach acknowledges that it's more important to share data than we agree on exactly how that data should be categorised, organised and named. We have given up on the idea that there is a single, knowable organization of the universe, a Book of Nature that we'll ever be able to read together or that will settle fights like the *Guinness Book of Records*.   (Weinberger, 2011, 149)

This raises important questions about evidential value both in the courts of law and the courts of history.

Lord David Neuberger, one of the United Kingdom's most distinguished jurists, has recently reflected on the law of torts, crucial in common law, where he argues that the law is more closely aligned to policy than principle:

> Thus, the point that there is little by way of hard and fast principle in the field of torts derives, I suggest, real support from the fact that analysis of tort cases, at least in the United Kingdom, appears to demonstrate a notable degree of disarray and a marked lack of reliable principle. First, there are some well-established principles which, on analysis, are hard to justify, and that makes one wonder about the value of having principles. Secondly, there are cases where apparently well-established principles

are subsequently disapproved and changed, which many may think is worse than having no principles in the first place. Thirdly, there are supposedly fundamental principles which then turn out to be subject to significant exceptions, which do not so much prove the rule as call the reliability of the rule into question. Fourthly, there are some principles which, while they are expressed as such by the courts, turn out, on analysis, to be so broadly expressed or so coarsely textured that they are, in truth, little, if anything, more than policy dressed up as principle. Fifthly, there are cases where the courts have grasped the nettle and accept that there is no clear principle and, depending on one's view, frankly or shamelessly base their decisions on policy.

(Neuberger, 2016)

Much the same could be said of what archivists grandly called principles that turn out on examination to be largely pragmatic, not enough storage space for example (Denning, 1966, 2), and driven, however reluctant they are to admit it, by policy. What is critical for at least the public archive, as Lord Neuberger, echoing his mentor Lord Bingham, has made crystal clear is that: 'The rule of law together with democracy is one of the two pillars on which our society is based. Therefore, if without good reason the media or anyone else undermines the judiciary, that risks undermining our society' (Croft, 2017).

Andrew Hoskins reminds us that it is impossible 'to return to an earlier, less risky, media age . . . This is obvious in the foolery known as "digital detox", whereby any period of abstinence from social media is always underpinned by the reassuring knowledge that discon-nection is only ever a temporary estrangement. We are already all addicts' (Hoskins, 2018, 2). And the figures bear him out. According to Internet Live Stats, about 40% of the world's population has internet access now.[12] Clearly, this can mean a number of things ranging from an iPhone in the pocket to accessing a shared internet connection in an African village, but we are pretty much all on the way to addiction.

If we are all part of a system to which we contribute even unwittingly, can we hope to archive it? In 2003, Oxford philosopher, Nick Bostrom, raised the intriguing possibility that we are all living in a computer simulation (Bostrom, 2003). While we may not wish to follow Bostrom's suggestion and go as far as to argue that the internet is simply the memory of a computer simulation, we certainly accept that the internet with its huge scale, its own rules and protocols, its own search tools and its enormous ability to mix the past and the present is an archive, if not *the* archive.

The ontology of the archive in the internet world

The concept of the archive as the internet or the internet as the archive marks a radical departure in thinking about the ontology of the archive, which ceases to be a cocooned and protected thing but, as Ernst and Hoskins suggest, free and organic. Long established curation practices that, as we have already described here and elsewhere, have been challenged in the analogue, are simply swept away (Moss, 2018, 253–79). Even the notion of fixity, long term preservation, is undermined as the internet repeatedly metamorphoses. Appraisal of physical content depends, in the majority of cases, on relatively well-organized record-keeping systems from which a choice can be made for permanent preservation. Irrespective of the approach, less than 5% of records created by the UK government found their way into the archives (Rock, 2017, 45–7). In some senses appraisal, as Groys has so firmly reminded us, is never absolute, but is permeable in what he terms the 'cultural economy':

> . . . the exchange that takes place between the archive of cultural values and the profane space outside of this archive. In the archive, things are collected and preserved that are regarded as being significant, relevant, and valuable for a certain culture. All other things that are regarded as being insignificant, irrelevant, and worthless remain in the profane space outside of the archive. Yet the cultural archives change constantly: some things from the profane space are incorporated, while others from the archive's collection are considered no longer relevant and sorted out.
>
> (Groys, 2012, 1)

Some have gone further in challenging the futility of archival practice, such as the artists Susan Hillier and Stephanie Gale who in their work 'create para-archives that juxtapose the archive and its ambitions to register the contingent with a set of objects for which there seems to be no assigned place in it, creating a series of supplements that question the foundations of archival hermeneutics' (Spicker, 2008, 175). On the internet this exchange happens constantly as content is uploaded, taken down, edited or reimagined. It was such transformation that the Wayback Machine sought to capture systematically in a fashion that had never been a feature of the analogue where the winnowing hand of time and interfering descendants and curators resulted in much being irretrievably lost.

The temporality of the archive in the internet world

If the internet has challenged the ontology of the archive, it has gone further in threatening the notion of the temporality of the archive. We have argued elsewhere that the traditional view of temporality in the archive was that enunciated by Lord Acton (1895, 45) in the late 19th century. For Acton, records moved from the court of law, where they were subject to the judgement of the courts, to the court of history, where they became subject to the judgement of historians. The distinction between the judgement of the courts and the judgement of historians was essentially that of fixity. Courts make single, final judgements, historians make provisional ones which are challenged, reviewed or swept away as new research or changes in historical fashions dictate.

In recent times, however, this clear distinction has been challenged for a range of reasons. The ending of double jeopardy for some crimes in England and Wales and the increased use of cold case reviews has meant that more records which were in the archival realm are being dragged back into the legal. Equally, reduced closure periods and Freedom of Information legislation have blurred the distinction between the two time periods.

However, it is the increased use of public inquiries to investigate tragedies in the past which has demolished the wall between Acton's two states. Inquiries such as those into Hillsborough, Bloody Sunday and the Iraq War have dragged material which was well on its way to the archives back into the judicial realm. In the case of Hillsborough, records of the tragedy were resting in the Sheffield archive before being dragged back as evidence before the Inquiry and then in a court of law (Moss and Thomas, 2017, 59).

The internet has blurred temporal boundaries and demolished fixity because it has brought the past much closer to the present, muddled them up and messed up the past. In the pre-internet era, the past was walled up in memory institutions – museums, television, video, archives. The internet has broken down these walls, ended decay time and begun to break down the distinction between the past and the present. As the cultural theorist Mark Fisher wrote in a chapter titled 'The Slow Cancellation of the Future' in his book *Ghosts of My Life*:

> If Kraftwerk's music came out of a casual intolerance of the already-established, then the present moment is marked by its extraordinary accommodation towards the past. More than that, the very distinction between past and present is breaking down. In 1981, the 1960s seemed much further away than they do today. Since then, cultural time has folded back on itself, and the impression of linear development has given way to a strange simultaneity.   (Fisher, 2014, 212)

He went on to foretell an 'existential regime that cyberspace will open up, where it is no longer necessary to physically move in order to access the whole history of culture. It will be there for us to discover from our mobile devices and desktops. We are told forever. It is remarkable how much old news is available in present time' (Fisher, 2014, 288).

Conclusion

King Wei of Chu, having heard of the ability of Zhuang Zhou, sent messengers with large gifts to bring him to his court, promising also that he would make him his chief minister. Zhuang Zhou, however, only laughed and said to them:

> A thousand ounces of silver are a great gain to me; and to be a high noble and minister is a most honourable position. But have you not seen the victim-ox for the border sacrifice? It is carefully fed for several years, and robed with rich embroidery that it may be fit to enter the Grand Temple. When the time comes for it to do so, it would prefer to be a little pig, but it cannot get to be so. Go away quickly, and do not soil me with your presence. I had rather amuse and enjoy myself in the midst of a filthy ditch than be subject to the rules and restrictions in the court of a sovereign.   (Horne, 1917, 397–8)

This is what the internet has done metaphorically to the archives, libraries and museums, which can no longer privilege information according to 'rules and restrictions in the court' (for which we might substitute the archive, library and museum professions), but allows people, 'even in the midst of a filthy ditch' from different cultures and perspectives to find and 'collect' information assemblages that are relevant and useful to them. As James Currall, Michael Moss and Susan Stuart (2006, 119) argued: 'We see the new information landscape as presenting information professions with new opportunities in relation to information availability and access, although it is clear that we will all have to be prepared to see information in new lights'. And, to answer our initial question, a Google search for Brewster Kahle returns 247,000 hits.

Notes

1   www.cinqueportsscribes.org.uk/gallery/triennial-project-2011-2013/
    the-last-word-poster-reduced-copy/#main.
2   www.cinqueportsscribes.org.uk/gallery/triennial-project-2011-2013/
    els-chrysalis/ #main.
3   http://vadimzakharov.conceptualism-moscow.org/page?id=
    1724&lang=en.
4   www.archive.org/about.
5   www.netpreserve.org/about-us.
6   www.geuzen.org/anxiety/installation, disabled in 2011 as Google
    changed its algorithms.
7   www.cyndislist.com/aboutus/#3.
8   www.cyndislist.com.
9   www.genealogyintime.com/articles/top-100-genealogy-websites-of-
    2016-page03. html.
10 www.geneabloggers.com/major-changes-geneabloggers.com.
11 www.socialmediagenealogy.com/genealogy-on-facebook-list.
12 www.internetlivestats.com/internet-users/#sources.

References

Acton, J.E.E.D. (Lord Acton) (1895) *Inaugural Lecture on the Study of History*,
    45.

Bostrom, N. (2003) Are We Living in a Computer Simulation?, *Philosophical Quarterly*, **53**, 243–55.

Cox, R. (2017) Farewell to AERI, or Last Words on the Archival Mission, www.readingarchivestheacademy.wordpress.com.

Croft, J. (2017) Neuberger attacks 'Enemies of the People' Criticism, *Financial Times*, 16 February.

Currall, J., Moss, M. and Stuart, S. (2006) Privileging Information is Inevitable, *Archives and Manuscripts*, **34** (1), 98–122.

Davies, W. (2017) Reasons for Corbyn, *London Review of Books*, **39** (14), 3-6.

Denning, A. (1966) *Report of the Committee on Legal Records, cmd. 3084*, HMSO.

Ernst, W. (2004) The Archive as Metaphor, *Open*, **7**, 46–53.

Evangelista, B. (2012) Brewster Kahle's Internet Archive, *San Francisco Chronicle*, 15 October.

Evans, S. (2010) The Archive in Theory: 'an archivist's fantasy gone mad'. In LIS 651-03: Prof. Irene Lopatovska, 2010, http://mysite.pratt.edu/~ilopatov/students/TheArchiveTheory-final.doc.

Fisher, M. (2014) *Ghosts of my Life: writings on depression, hauntology and lost futures*, Zero Books.

Giles, H. (1926) *Chuang Tzŭ: Mystic, Moralist and Social Reformer*, Bernard Quaritch.

Gray, N. (2015) RDF, the Semantic Web, Jordan, Jordan and Jordan. In Moss, M., Endicott-Popovsky, B. and Dupuis, M. J. (eds), *Is Digital Different? How Information Creation, Capture, Preservation and Discovery are Being Transformed*, Facet Publishing.

Groys, B. (Strathausen, C. (trans.)) (2012) *Under Suspicion: a phenomenology of media*, Columbia University Press.

Harris, V. (2002) The Archival Sliver: power, memory, and archives in South Africa, *Archival Science*, **2**, 63–86.

Holland, T. (2007) *The Archivist's Story*, Random House.

Horne, C. F. (ed.) (1917) *The Sacred Books and Early Literature of the East, Vol. XII: Medieval China*.

Hoskins, A. (2013) The End of Decay Time, *Memory Studies*, **6** (4), 387–9.

Hoskins, A. (2014) The Mediatization of Memory. In Lundby, K. (ed.), *Mediatization of Communication*, De Gruyter Mouton.

Hoskins, A. (2016) Archive Me! Media, Memory, Uncertainty. In Hajek, A., Lohmeier, C. and Pentzold, C., *Memory in a Mediated World*, Springer, 13–35.

Hoskins, A. (2018, forthcoming) The Restless Past: introduction to digital memory and media. In Hoskins, A. (ed.), *Digital Memory Studies: media pasts in transition*, Routledge. We are grateful to Professor Hoskins for allowing us to see a pre-print of his paper.

Karpf, D. (2012) Social Science Research Methods in Internet Time, *Information, Communication & Society*, **15** (5), 640; (quoted in Hoskins, 2014).

Kassow, S.D. (2007) *Who Will Write Our History: Emanuel Ringelblum, the Warsaw Ghetto, and the Oyneg Shabes Archive*, Indiana University Press.

Keene, D. (2008) Interview with Derek Keene, *Making History*, 2008, www.history.ac.uk/makinghistory/resources/interviews/ Keene_Derek.html.

Lepore, J. (2015) The Cobweb: can the internet be archived, *The New Yorker*, 26 January.

Levy, D. M. (2011) *Scrolling Forward: making sense of documents in the digital age*, Arcade Publishing.

Library of Congress (2017), private communication to David Thomas.

Mayer-Schönberger, V. (2009) *Delete: the virtue of forgetting in the digital age*, Princeton University Press.

Moore, N., Salter, A., Stanley, L. and Tamboukou, M. (2017) *The Archive Project: archival research in the social sciences*, Routledge, quoting Michel de Certeau (1998) *The Writing of History*, Columbia University Press.

Moss, M. and Thomas, D. (2017) Overlapping Temporalities – the judge, the historian and the citizen, *Archives*, **52**, 134, 51–66.

Moss, M. (2018) Memory Institutions, The Archive and Digital Disruption? In Hoskins, A. (ed.), *Digital Memory Studies: media pasts in transition*, Routledge.

Neuberger, D. (2016) Some Thoughts on the Principles Governing the Law of Torts, *New Jurist Magazine*, 21 November.

Negroponte, N. (1991) Products and Services for Computer Networks, *Scientific American*, **265** (3), 106–13.

Nora, P. (1989) Between Memory and History: les lieux de mémoire, *Representations*, **26**, 7–25.

Nowotny, H. (1994) *Time: The Modern and Postmodern Experience*, Polity Press.

Osterberg, G. (2013) Update on the Twitter Archive at the Library of Congress, *Library of Congress Blog*, January 4.

Reading, A. (2011) The London Bombings: mobile witnessing, mortal bodies and globital time, *Memory Studies*, 2009, **4** (3), 298–311.

Rock, P. (2017) The Dreadful Flood of Documents: the 1958 Public Record Act and its aftermath, Part 2: After-Effects, *Archives*, **52** (134), 26–50.

Spicker, S. (2008) *The Big Archive: art from bureaucracy*, MIT Press.

Stille, A. (2002) *The Future of the Past – how the information age threatens to destroy our cultural heritage*, Picador.

The top 100 Genealogy list, *Genealogyintime*, 2016, http://www.genealogyintime.com/articles/top-100-genealogy-websites-of-2016-page03.html.

Weinberger, D. (2011) *Too Big to Know*, Basic Books.

Zimmer, M. (2015) The Twitter Archive at the Library of Congress: challenges for information practice and information policy, *First Monday*, 6 July.

Acknowledgements

Michael Moss is Professor of Archival Science at Northumbria University, where David Thomas is a Visiting Professor. They would like to thank Liza Dimbleby for the Brezhnev reference, Louise Craven for drawing our attention to Richard Cox's blog, Andrew Hoskins for his help and advice, Nicolas Malevé for the link to De Geuzen, Els Van Den Steen for permission to cite and reproduce her work and David Weinberger to quote his work.

9

The end of archival ideas?

Craig Gauld

The central structure of this chapter is indebted to Robert Rowland-Smith, consultant, writer and lecturer on philosophy, literature and psychoanalysis. In 2015, he argued that we are coming to the end of the Age of Ideas. In doing so, he examined how different 'ages' – of superstition, religion, reason and ideas – have emerged and gradually been eclipsed. His Ages of Reason and Ideas, and their subsequent deaths, chimed with thoughts the author had been having about the archival sphere and have been co-opted here.

(Rowland-Smith, 2015)

Introduction

Caroline Brown, in the introduction to *Archives and Recordkeeping: Theory into Practice*, began with the following quotation from Anthony Kenny's *A New History of Western Philosophy*:

> Thomas Carlyle . . . was once reproached by a businessman for being too interested in mere ideas. 'There was once a man called Rousseau', Carlyle replied, 'who wrote a book containing nothing but ideas. The second edition was bound in the skins of those who laughed at the first'.
> (Brown, 2014, xi)

This quotation was used as a tool to lead into the professional schism that exists within the recordkeeping community between theory and practice. The stated purpose of the book was to 'demonstrate the value of thinking about theory and its relationship with the practical world' (Brown, 2014, xi). That there was a need for a publication with such a purpose is strange because we have, as a profession, fallen in love with ideas. Since the middle of the 1970s – from around the time of the publication of F. G. Ham's 'The Archival Edge' and the creation of the *Archivaria* journal in 1975 – the archival community has embraced innovative ideas and theories. Whilst this is not to suggest that no previous innovation or theoretical thinking impacted on the profession prior to 1975 – Theodore Schellenberg, for example, revolutionised the profession in the immediate aftermath of World War II with his ideas of primary and secondary value (Schellenberg, 1956) – it is to recognise that the entwining of professional progression with theory, post-1975, subsequently moved the profession away from a conception of itself as insular, neutral and focused only on facilitating the outputs of historians, to that of Archival Science – the autonomous scientific discipline that covers theory, methodology and practice and encapsulates and expresses the importance of what it is that archivists and recordkeepers do. However, it is the contention of this chapter that what will be characterised as an Age of Archival Ideas is dead. Put succinctly, ideas in the archival sphere are past their prime in an Age of Information.

Definitions

For the purposes of this argument, what is meant by an 'idea'? The dictionary definition of an idea is 'a thought or suggestion about a possible course of action' (OUP, 2001, 442). In archival literature, there has been a tendency to discuss theories rather than ideas; the definition of theory is 'an idea or sets of ideas that is intended to explain something' (OUP, 2001, 943). Whilst there is an external body of thought that distinguishes between theory and idea, this chapter uses the words interchangeably, understanding ideas and theories slightly differently to be figments or speculative framings, often, although not necessarily, without a connection to physical reality. Viewing them in this way helps us to move beyond an archival Burkean positivism and the requirement for theories or ideas to be tested in practice so as to '[be] entered into the canon of archival thought and take their places as *immutable laws of the profession* [author's italics]' (Burke, 1981, 42).

Whilst advocacy of universal laws is distinctly old-fashioned in the 21st century, what Burke is really forwarding is the notion of prevailing ideas (Rowland-Smith, 2015). These are not always active in our minds, but they form the context for our culture and inform our assumptions. For example, some prevailing archival ideas could include the principles of provenance/*respect des fonds* and original order. Prevailing ideas shape our attitudes, practices and educational, professional and ethical frameworks, if not quite being universal laws.

Therefore, prevailing ideas are not innovative or new in the way that, for example, the Records Continuum model or the application of postmodernism within an archival context was in the post-1975 period. It is such innovative ideas that this chapter is referring to when stating that we have fallen in, and subsequently out of, love with ideas.

From an archival Age of Reason to an archival Age of Ideas

The archival profession does not operate in a vacuum and the move towards ideas mimicked changes in society (albeit a little behind the times – the archive profession is not one that could often be said to be cutting-edge). The counterculture movement of the 1960s spawned a plethora of ideas emerging from a new generation of disaffected, radicalised young people. From a freedom to focus beyond the provision of material necessities came a confluence of cultural ideas around human sexuality, women's rights, ethnicity and traditional modes of authority and power relations that moved away from prevalent cultural mores (Patterson, 1996, 306–14). This decade was a demonstration of the leading role that ideas can play in the orientation of society and it subsequently had a seismic effect on the archive and the role of the archivist, via archival theorists drawing on and co-opting aspects of what came to be known as postmodernist theory. According to the *Encyclopedia of World Problems & Human Potential*:

> While encompassing a broad range of ideas, postmodernism is typically defined by an attitude of scepticism, irony or distrust toward grand narratives, ideologies and various tenets of universalism, including objective notions of reason, human nature, social progress, moral universalism, absolute truth, and objective reality.
> 08.11.2017, http://encyclopedia.uia.org/en/problem/136818.

Archives, up to this point, had been, like many other cultural institutions, a product of Enlightenment rationality. Institutions such as the Public Records Office of the United Kingdom, formed in 1838, and publications such as Muller, Feith and Fruin's *Manual for the Arrangement and Description of Archives*, published in 1898, or Hilary Jenkinson's *A Manual of Archive Administration*, published in 1922, emerged from the encyclopedic spirit of the Age of Reason and from notions that everything in the universe could be rationally demystified and catalogued. This archive was rooted in scientific and historical enquiry, a discourse resting upon a set of techniques appropriated to proclaim with a measure of validity an approximation of the truth and an accurate representation of the world. Formative archival concepts such as provenance, original order, context and custody made it easy to tell the story of the past without conjecture. In this version of the archive, time slows down and the important facts slide along to the historian like suitcases on a conveyor belt at an airport; you pick them, put them on the page, and the job of writing factual history is done. Archivists, therefore, were impeccable custodians of history: 'the most selfless devotee of Truth the modern world produces' (Jenkinson, 1944, 16), gatekeepers to the maze within which seekers would lose themselves to the glories held within.

For archival postmodernists, or those simply influenced by postmodernist discourse, such faith in the archive and the archivist was untenable, 'at best outdated, at worst inherently dangerous' in the words of Elisabeth Kaplan (2000, 147). The postmodernist turn represented a predominantly theoretical shift in emphasis towards meaning(s) and away from positivist epistemology. In emphasising 'the casual and socially constitutive role of cultural processes and systems of signification' (Steinmetz, 1999, 1–2) there was an implicit recognition that society was a construct and not as it was presented. It was messier, there were truths rather than Truth, what was revealed was not objective fact but subjective selection and so on.

Hence the shift towards a questioning, theoretical, archival profession that emerged in the middle of the 1970s was an instance of individuals recognising practical failings, becoming self-conscious and asking each other: What are Archives? What is an Archivist? In so doing, a sector of the profession became liberated from the pure practicalities of a practical profession. They inherently understood that often ideas are not real; that, by definition, ideas are mental speculations that tend to reside in a realm above day-to-day realities and practicalities; that without conceptualisation of an alternative that is not a replication of current reality it is virtually impossible for better realities to come into being.

Postmodernism operated on a plain above the day-to-day practicalities of archiving however. As a result of its influence, the archival community became consumed by new and intellectually challenging ideas that propelled the profession forward via radical thought experiments that sought to overturn past certainties. This Age of Archival Ideas was the period of Terry Cook and Verne Harris; of Postmodernism and the Records Continuum model; of Jacques Derrida and Michel Foucault becoming staples of archival literature; of social justice and representation agendas coming to the fore; of culture and community; of politics, power and subjectivity; of the voiceless and the dispossessed; of archival intellectualisation and internationalisation; of the activist archivist; of professionalisation; and the emergence and solidification of what is known as Archival Science.

The end of archival ideas in an age of information

Why, then, the claim that this Age of Archival Ideas is dead? Firstly, the Age of Archival Ideas was founded upon an emerging body of theoretical archival literature that publicised the subversive thinking that was being undertaken and the revolution (or paradigm shift) that was taking place in Archival Science. The body of new, cutting-edge theoretical work that seeks to radically alter the outlook and practice of the archival profession has, however, thinned considerably in the last decade. Admittedly such a claim may appear strange at this present time; for example, we have a flourishing publishing industry with several publishing houses seeking to initiate publications that deal in-depth with aspects of archival theory. In addition, there has been work published and undertaken recently that conceives of an archival alternative that is not simply a replication of current reality but envisions better realities to come. For example, the considerable and expanding literature on Community Archives, coupled with its practical implementation, which is being driven by people such as Andrew Flinn (2007), is both questioning and having a deep and long-lasting impact on the nature of the archive and what our role as archivists should be.

Yet, if you were asked to name the archival theorists who first come to mind then you would most likely come up with something along the lines of Terry Cook, Verne Harris, Eric Ketelaar, Brien Brothman, Tom Nesmith, Frank Upward, Sue McKemmish, Jeanette Bastian and Randall Jimerson. These theorists have for several years been using postmodernism and critical theories (Sue McKemmish acknowledged the influence of postmodernist musings on the Records Continuum (McKemmish, 2001, 347)) to construct a particular archival knowledge base and have all contributed to a paradigm that forms a loosely assembled carapace above us that unquestionably shapes our attitudes. Their ideas serve as our frame of reference; they have become the authors of the prevailing ideas of the profession and the work of Flinn, for example, slots neatly into their narrative.

It is not to do the names on this list a disservice, however, to state that these authors produced their main ideas, in some cases pioneering ideas for the profession, a number of years ago. Jimerson, whose main publication *Archives Power: memory, accountability and social justice* (Jimerson, 2009), represented, in the words of Dr Patricia Whatley, 'sustained research over 20 years' (Society of American Archivists, https://saa.archivists.org/store/archives-power-memory-accountability-and-social-justice/1354/) and arose out of many similar arguments forwarded in prior journal articles (Jimerson, 2006 and 2007). Yet, so successful and ubiquitous have their ideas become that a cosy professional consensus has kicked-in with regards to what we can loosely term a democratisation or social justice agenda (Greene, 2013; Gauld, 2017). As a result, many journal articles written today represent a continuation of long-standing themes emergent from the pages of the aforementioned theorists rather than radical new ideas. They tend to seek to display how one archive or another has undertaken actions to support the processes of democratisation over the past couple of decades, opening the archive up to an increased number of users whilst democratising a set of processes that were previously elitist, closed off, inaccessible and representative of a societal power imbalance.

This is not to undermine the perspective of those articles that document progressive intentions, yet it is curious that, at a time of expanding numbers of archival graduates emerging from programmes around the world and increasing interdisciplinarity, the extent of genuinely new or critical thinking emerging from within the archival profession that challenges these current prevailing orthodoxies or seeks to change the archival direction of travel appears to be contracting in contrast to that coming from outside the profession – particularly the thought-provoking and creative work found, for example, in *The Archive Project: archival research in the social sciences* (Moore et al., 2016).

However, having previously stated that archives do not operate in a vacuum, the author would suggest that the demise of ideas in an archival context is not occurring in isolation. There is a wider shift taking place whereby ideas in general society are, today, quite simply not what they used to be. This is a thought that has been forwarded by Neil Gabler, Senior Fellow at the University of Southern California:

> Once upon a time, they could ignite fires of debate, stimulate other thoughts, incite revolutions and fundamentally change the way we look and think about the world. They could penetrate the general culture and make celebrities out of thinkers.   (Gabler, 2011)

No longer. What we see today are experts ridiculed (YouTube, 2016), celebrities feted as great thinkers (Ellis-Petersen, 2015) and the rise of reactionaries. At the time of writing, Donald J. Trump is the President of the United States; Marine Le Pen made it to the run-off of the French Presidential Election in April 2017; the far-right, nationalist AfD have made gains in German parliamentary elections (September 2017), winning 12.6% of the vote; and religious extremism is terrorising large parts of the globe in the form of Daesh/ISIS. A history of the demise of ideas within society is too complex for a chapter of this length however, as Gabler (2011) outlines, 'we live in a society that no longer thinks big'. Instead, we live in a post-idea society where people do not think at all:

> In effect, we are living in an increasingly post-ideas world – a world in which big, thought-provoking ideas that can't be instantly monetised are of so little intrinsic value that fewer people are generating them and fewer outlets are disseminating them, the internet notwithstanding. Bold ideas are almost passé.   (Gabler, 2011)

Gabler goes on to attack some obvious modern tools, Twitter for example. Attacking them individually does not, for this author, achieve anything nor get to the root of any problem. However, he is on to something when he argues that the problem is information itself: the Information Age is simply dangerous for ideas. This may appear counter-intuitive for a generation that has the level of information at our fingertips that we do. However, as Paul Virilio cautioned in 1995, 'What will be gained from electronic information and electronic communication will necessarily result in a loss elsewhere' (Virilio, 1995). What has seemingly been lost is the ability to contextualise information. As Gabler states:

> In the past, we collected information to convert it into something larger than facts (or alternative facts) and ultimately more useful – into ideas that made sense of the information. We sought not just to apprehend the world but to truly comprehend it, which is really the primary function of ideas.
> (Gabler, 2011)

Our ability to stand back and to assess where the information came from, to ascertain its authenticity and veracity, to question rather than digest, has been diminished in this argument. This, with the rise of Donald Trump, fake news and the post-truth society, is now seen in many instances as a virtue (BBC Trending, 2016; D'Ancona, 2017, 7–34). Hence, we prefer knowing to thinking because knowing has more immediate value. It keeps us in the loop, keeps us connected to our friends and our cohorts within our self-made silos or safe spaces where we can communicate only with those we consider 'good' or 'virtuous' (Tett, 2015, 12–16).

Additionally, this information universe has changed the game for information professionals as having such quantities of information at our fingertips has made us come to expect, as consumers, instant results. The consumer is the central figure in twenty-first century discourse and marks a shift from passive recipient to active choice-maker in relation to service provision. The archival profession has been unable to stand apart from this. Technology has shifted the power away from the organization and the information professional towards the individual user. As stewards of cultural materials, archives have always managed access to, and use of, their collections, but the digital environment is radically changing cultural consumption and production patterns, obliging archives to re-think how they relate to their audiences as users of cultural content.

More and more, users are expecting that the effort it takes to undertake research within an archive be lessened. The community expects its information sources to be available online and increasingly regards anything that is not online as being irrelevant. For funders, this market language of use and efficiencies is key whilst an ethos of managerialism strips the ethical and moral away from public services. Hence, it becomes more difficult to display the relevance of archives and archivists in the 21st century. Cultural gatekeepers are dispensable; physical, hard copy access to records is passé as people want online only; the digital archive is a nebulous concept at the heart of which lie Information Technologists rather than Information Professionals, and so on.

This is reflected in the perilous financial situation many publicly funded archives find themselves in in the United Kingdom. Although it is difficult in the UK to ascertain authoritative figures as local authority and publicly funded archives operate in a very diverse sector, with many also subsumed within library services and larger heritage services, we do know that 'public bodies [were] dealing with cuts to their budgets of between 25 and 40%' according to *Archives of the 21st Century in Action: refreshed 2012–15* (The National Archives, 2012). This document has now been superseded by *Archives Unlocked: Releasing the Potential* (The National Archives, 2017). Avoiding the anodyne title and its insinuation that the profession has been failing to fulfil its potential all these years, it is interesting that amidst the discussions of releasing this potential and think-pieces on the archival direction of travel, there is nothing on cuts or current funding and staffing levels that would enable the action plan to be implemented effectively. This suggests that the situation has not improved.

It may be that this, and the call in the Ministerial Foreword for a future 'in which businesses, creative industries, arts organisations, academic, and communities can fully *exploit* [author's italics] archives' (The National Archives, 2017, 1) is illustrative. As a consequence, archives are having to fight tooth-and-nail to remain viable in this environment. The *Archives Unlocked* document outlined the following as key points for action going forward:

- Develop the **digital capacity** of the archive sector, to preserve digital records and increase discoverability of the paper and digital archive.
- Build the sector's **resilience** to ensure more archives can meet and sustain the Archive Service Accreditation standard, open the sector to

new skills and a more diverse workforce, increase income generation capacities, and support innovative service models.

- Demonstrate the **impact** of archives by developing and expanding audiences, piloting approaches to using data and evidence, and influencing thinking in the IT, commercial and knowledge sectors.

(The National Archives, 2017, 17)

These follow on from similar action points in the preceding *Archives of the 21st Century in Action* document which coalesced around similar core themes of access, inclusion and digitisation. Hence, it is understandable if ideas that seek to radically alter are not relevant at a time of extreme technological, societal and financial pressure where the profession must focus on concrete goals linked to government strategies simply to prove its worth, or unlock its potential, rather than engaging with, or developing, radical new conceptions of professional practice. The focus, therefore, is on developing a more symbiotic relationship with our users in that we shape services more to their needs and expectations; becoming increasingly flexible in our approaches to preserving records in both centralised and distributed custodial settings; digitising collections that have the most worth, both in terms of use and monetarisation; designing user interfaces that take into account different user expectations; and, at the extreme, reducing archives purely to data so as to save money on storage.

The future of the profession?

Despite scepticism amongst some practitioners (Hunt, 2009, 10), ideas and theories have fundamentally changed the profession from that which existed in 1975, even if day-to-day practitioners do not fully realise it or even if recordkeeping does not fully conform to the prescriptions set out within these ideas. The reason archivists are engaging in day-to-day, taken-for-granted activities such as outreach initiatives, connecting, liaising and assisting community archives, being involved in the design of the organizational EDRMS, or, if students, being taught about recordkeeping rather than just archive management or records management, is due to the ideas set out by the pioneering archival thinkers that came before us. As a result, we must, as a profession, recognise the role that ideas and theories can play in such a practice-based discipline: there is nothing wrong with being interested in 'mere ideas'.

However, if an Age of Archival Ideas is dead, as this author suggests, does this mean that the Archival Science race is run? Are we useless in the absence of new ideas, an ever-diminishing intellectual and professional life force? Categorically, the answer is no. Ultimately, an assertion that an Age of Archival Ideas is dead is clearly a provocative observation open to the accusation of hyperbole and could be viewed as innately pessimistic in that it points to a lack of intellectualisation or critical thinking. This is not, of course, the case. It is rather to suggest that energies and attentions are generally directed elsewhere into more 'practical' matters, ensuring that we become, in the eyes of the Government, inclusive and accessible organizations (Department for Media, Culture and Sport, 2000), or assisting in the development of digitisation solutions that will increase access to the historical record.

These are valid and important concerns and provide short-term value in ensuring that we can provide visible evidence of immediate work undertaken that can play within predominately Governmental strategies – a practice-based discipline focusing on practical outcomes and relevance at a time of extreme hardship is unavoidable. Also, it does need to be qualified that an age 'past' is not an age expunged and that many of the ideas and concepts that emerged post-1975 are alive and active within the prevailing framework of archival discourse and practice. Nor does it mean that original and radical ideas and theories will not emerge within archival literature going forward but, rather, that the importance invested in them by the profession will not be comparable to its golden age as professional focus will continue to be directed, correctly, elsewhere.

However, it does feel that a seismic change has taken place within the archival profession and we have reached 'peak-theory'. Before, it was a common lament in certain quarters that individual practitioners simply did not have time to be interested in theory and ideas. As Brown writes:

> . . . for many, faced with the day-to-day realities of managing the records, people and resources in their care, dealing with managers and stakeholders, and keeping in check the relentless tide of e-mails, there is little time for consideration of the big picture.   (Brown, 2014, xi)

Today, however, it seems that the challenges facing us are so great that the impracticality or irrelevance of ideas envelops the overarching whole. How are we to react or compete when Google's mission statement is to 'organise the world's information and make it universally accessible and useful' (Google)? This is the biggest idea going in the 21st century and it comes from the technological behemoth that sits astride access to information on the World Wide Web. In this scenario, the internet is literally the archive:

> . . . a repository of material which has only been loosely classified, material whose status is as yet indeterminate and stands between rubbish, junk and significance: material that has not yet been read and researched.   (Featherstone, 2006, 594)

In this environment, we are hanging on by our fingertips, seeking to find a foothold in this disorientating Age of Information whilst trying to ignore the elephant in the room that is that it is all futile anyway as Artificial Intelligence in the form of algorithms will be doing all our jobs for us in 30 years (Theimer, 2016).

So, what is to be done? To return to Brown:

> Arguing about and working towards an understanding of what archives and records are, what recordkeepers do and why they do it is one of the elements that contributes to our status as a profession.
>   (Brown, 2014, xvii)

Indeed. However, it is the belief of this author that too much conversation tends to take place criticising the nature of the archive and, more specifically, the role of the archivist. For a number of years, wading through professional literature or attending professional conferences has felt like an exercise in self-flagellation, where postmodernist critiques, some of which were appropriate when first communicated, are repeated and repeated ad nauseam. It can be rather draining, for all the virtues and good intentions inherent in the ideas, to be continually told how we as archivists are to blame for all manner of documentary ills; how the profession could be 'inherently dangerous'; how admitting one's failings and exposing our personal or political biases is more important than acting professionally and aiming for as close to neutrality or objectivity as is within our capabilities; and how there is no such thing as 'fact' or 'truth'.

Perhaps what is needed now is not that we retract even further into ourselves, becoming nothing more than a talking-shop or echo chamber in the face of the most fundamental challenges the profession has faced since becoming professionalised, continually talking and debating what we do, what we ought to do and how important we are to key agendas of the day. Instead, we need to stop being sheepish and reach a professional consensus that recognises and understands that what we do as guardians of the evidence on which an individual's or societal truth can be established is a valid statement of professional practice and is of substantial value. Evidence, cared for properly, in context, can proclaim an *approximation* of the truth. As Terry Eastwood wrote:

> Archival documents do capture a moment in time, fix and freeze it, as it were, in order to preserve some sense of it for future reference, some sense of the unique character of the actions and events from which the documents arose. (Eastwood, 1993, 112)

Therefore, our core professional tenets and competencies, those that have underpinned us since the days of the *Manual of Archival Administration*, have a place in the 21st century. We need to mount a spirited defence of the archive and to communicate it loudly and proudly beyond our professional boundaries.

Indeed, we do not need to look far to find inspiration. Recent developments in the United States with Donald Trump and the United Kingdom via Brexit have brought with them a call to find added value in the archive and the reassertion of concepts such as facts and evidence and truth – concepts that should be at the core of what we think we are doing as archivists. In this environment, there is a place for someone who seeks to be 'professional', displaying trust-worthiness, possessing appropriate specialist knowledge and skills, and aspiring to excellence (Cogan, 1953). In acting in this manner, the archive can be a conduit through which authentic and reliable records of evidence can be used to deduce what has happened. As Heather MacNeil has outlined, a philosophical ideal of truth emerges from a philosophy of rational belief based on probability:

> Assent to any proposition was to be based on the strength of the evidence, that is, on the strength of the connection between the proposition to be proved and the material offered as proof; and there was a new emphasis on the grading of evidence on the scales of reliability and probable truth. Hence, the truth of any proposition could be established by reasoning from the relevant evidence, with reason operating within a framework of inferences, generalisation and probabilities.
>
> (MacNeil, 2001, 38)

It would seem to me that this lay behind the post-Brexit posting by Margaret Proctor on an archival list-serv (Proctor, 2016). Whilst disagreeing with her overarching analysis that the vote was a 'failure in education, in information dissemination', suggesting that those who voted out were anti-intellectuals who did not have the full facts (or bother to find them out), it is clear to me that 'Evidence – authentic, accessible and contextualised' is key to improving the democratic processes of the future and could be a clarion call for all professionals and professional action. Indeed, the Latin roots of the term *evidentem* is 'perceptible, clear, obvious' (Online Etymology Dictionary), reinforcing the need for evidence as a counter-point to those who seek to mislead and misinform.

Conclusion

The response of the archival community must be to work within traditional principles and parameters and, more concretely, embed these principles and parameters – these prevailing ideas, if you will – within archival solutions to digital problems. Should a societal backlash to the misuse of information continue and flourish then it may be that we will see an increased validation of the archival role with a move to re-contextualisation, with the digital environment and its myriad of avenues and never-ending choices leading to greater demands for re-intermediation, involving contextual framing and the archival intermediary. This is precisely the area that an individual like Geoffrey Yeo is working in, with his investigations into the nature of the record in the digital environment (Yeo, 2007, 2012, 2014, 2017) and:

... how, in digital realms, we can and should embrace the potential for granular or item-oriented approaches that will support contextualisation but will also allow users to assemble and reassemble their own aggregations in ways that respond to their differing needs and perceptions.

(Yeo, http://www.ucl.ac.uk/dis/people/geoffreyyeo/research)

In addition, there are, for example, those such as Luciana Duranti and her work on digital forensics (Duranti and Endicott-Popovsky, 2010) and Victoria Lemieux on blockchain and the value of its technology in creating and preserving trustworthy records (Lemieux, 2016). What Yeo, Duranti and Lemieux are doing, as individuals, is finding forward-thinking, innovative, practical resolutions to ensure that the archival profession can remain relevant over the next 30 years with its traditional principles and integrity intact. Work such as this presents the best hope we have of ensuring the long-term preservation of the profession and enabling the archivist, and the principles we hold dear, to endure in the digital domain. By so doing, they, and others, may create professional space for the radical archival ideas of the future.

References

BBC Trending (2016) The Rise and Rise of Fake News, www.bbc.co.uk/news/blogs-trending-37846860.

Brown, C. (2014) Introduction. In Brown, C. (ed.), *Archives and Recordkeeping: theory into practice*, Facet Publishing.

Burke, F. G. (1981) The Future of Archival Theory in the United States, *American Archivist*, **44** (1), 40–46.

Cogan, M. L. (1953) Toward a Definition of Profession, *Harvard Education Review*, **23**, 33–50.

D'Ancona, M. (2017) *Post-Truth: the new war on truth and how to fight back*, Ebury Press.

Department for Media, Culture and Sport (2000) *Centres for Social Change: museums, galleries and archives for all*, http://webarchive.nationalarchives.gov.uk/20100113222743/http:/www.cep.culture.gov.uk/images/publications/centers_social_change.pdf.

Duranti, L. and Endicott-Popovsky, B. (2010) Digital Records Forensics: a new science and academic program for forensic readiness, *Journal of*

Digital Forensics, Security and Law, **5** (2), 45–62.

Eastwood, T. (1993) How Goes it with Appraisal, *Archivaria,* **36**, 111–21.

Ellis-Petersen, H. (2015) Russell Brand Voted World's Fourth Most Influential Thinker, *The Guardian,* 26 March, www.theguardian.com/culture/2015/mar/26/hot-prospect-russell-brand-voted-worlds-fourth-most-influential-thinker.

Featherstone M. (2006) Archive, *Theory, Culture and Society,* **23**, 591–6.

Flinn, A. (2007) Community Histories, Community Archives: some opportunities and challenges, *Journal of the Society of Archivists,* **28** (2), 151–76.

Gabler, N. (2011) The Elusive Big Idea, *New York Times,* 13 August, www.nytimes.com/2011/08/14/opinion/sunday/the-elusive-big-idea.html?_r=0.

Gauld, C. (2017) Democratising or Privileging: the democratisation of knowledge and the role of the archivist, *Archival Science,* **17** (3), 227–45.

Google, About us, www.google.com/about/company.

Greene, M. (2013) A Critique of Social Justice as an Archival Imperative: what is it we're doing that's all that important?, *American Archivist,* **76** (2), 302–34.

Ham, F. G. (1975) The Archival Edge, *American Archivist,* **38** (1), 5–13.

Hunt, R. (2009) Starting Out: the thoughts of this year's students on the MARM course, *ARC Magazine,* **233**, 10.

Jenkinson, H. (1944) British Archives and the War, *American Archivist,* **7**, 1–17.

Jimerson, R. (2006) Embracing the Power of Archives, *American Archivist,* **69** (1), 19–32.

Jimerson, R. (2007) Archives for All: professional responsibility and social justice, *American Archivist,* **70** (2), 252–81.

Jimerson, R. (2009) *Archives Power: memory, accountability and social justice,* Society of American Archivists.

Kaplan, E. (2000) We Are What We Collect, We Collect What We Are: archives and the construction of identity, *American Archivist,* **63**, 126–51.

Lemieux, V. (2016) Trusting Records: is blockchain technology the answer?, *Records Management Journal,* **26** (2), 110–39.

MacNeil, H. (2001) Trusting Records in a Postmodern World, *Archivaria,* **51**, 36–47.

McKemmish, S. (2001) Placing Records Continuum Theory and Practice, *Archival Science,* **1** (4), 333–59.

Moore, N., Salter, A., Stanley, L. and Tamboukou, M. (2016) *The Archive*

Project: archival research in the social sciences, Routledge.

Online Etymology Dictionary, Evident,
www.etymonline.com/search?q=evidentem.

Oxford University Press (2001) *Compact Oxford Dictionary Thesaurus and Wordpower Guide,* Oxford University Press.

Patterson, J. T. (1996) *Grand Expectations: The United States, 1945–1974,* Oxford University Press.

Proctor, M. (2016) EU Referendum – A Personal Reflection, *Archives-NRA List-Serv.*

Rowland-Smith, R. (2015) The End of the Age of Ideas, *Radio 4,* www.bbc.co.uk/programmes/b0643t65.

Schellenberg, T. (1956) *Modern Archives,* Chicago Press.

Steinmetz, G. (1999) *State/Culture: state-formation after the cultural turn,* Cornell University Press.

Tett, G. (2015) *The Silo Effect: why putting everything in its place isn't such a bright idea,* Little, Brown.

The Encyclopedia of World Problems and Human Potential, Postmodernism, http://encyclopedia.uia.org/en/problem/136818.

The National Archives (2012) *Archives for the 21st Century in Action: refreshed 2012–15,* www.nationalarchives.gov.uk/documents/archives/ archives21centuryrefreshed-final.pdf.

The National Archives (2017) *Archives Unlocked: releasing the potential,* www.nationalarchives.gov.uk/documents/archives/Archives-Unlocked-Brochure.pdf.

Theimer, K. (2016) My #ACA2016 Plenary: it's the end of the archival profession as we know it, and I feel fine, 14 June, www.archivesnext.com/?p=4031.

Virilio, P. (1995) Speed and Information: cyberspace alarm!, *CTHEORY.NET,* www.ctheory.net/ctheory_wp/speed-and-information-cyberspace-alarm-2.

Yeo, G. (2007) Concepts of Record (1): evidence, information, and persistent representations, *American Archivist,* **71**, 118–43.

Yeo, G. (2012) Bringing Things Together: aggregate records in a digital age, *Archivaria,* **74**, 43–91.

Yeo, G. (2014) Contexts, Originals, and Item-Level Orientation: responding creatively to users' needs and technological change, *Journal of Archival Organization,* **12** (3–4), 170–85.

Yeo, G. (2017) Continuing Debates about Description. In Eastwood, T. and

MacNeil, H. (eds), *Currents of Archival Thinking*, Libraries Unlimited.
YouTube (2016) Gove: Britons 'have had enough of experts',
   www.youtube.com/watch?v=GGgiGtJk7MA.

Index